This Book Belongs to:

_____

Published with a generous grant from the Xeric Foundation
www.xericfoundation.com

Distributed in association with AdHouse Books
The AdHouse logo is © 2005 AdHouse Books
www.adhousebooks.com

www.bumperboy.net
debbie@bumperboy.net

ISBN: 0-9766610-0-4
10 9 8 7 6 5 4 3 2 1

First Printing, June 2005
Printed in Canada

DEDICATED TO:
Mom, Dad, Pam, Scott, Cindy, Mike, Sean, Vicky, & Ben.
I love you all!

MANY THANKS TO:
Chris Pitzer, James Sime and the Isotope, the Xeric Foundation, Keith Knight, my friends, my family, my idols, and Bumperboy's fans, for their support, encouragement, and kindness.

BUMPERBOY

loses his marbles!

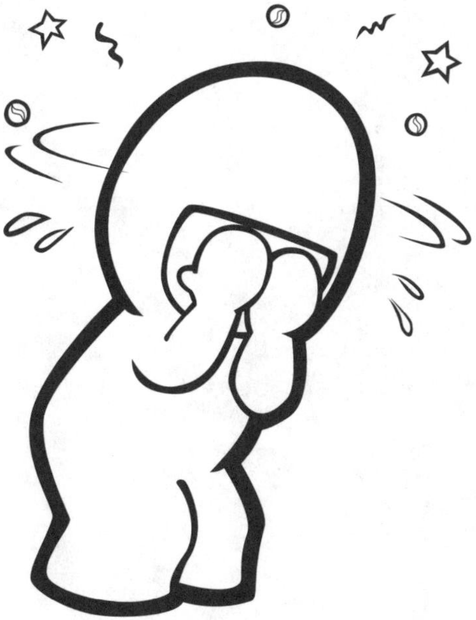

BY DEBBIE HUEY

PART ONE

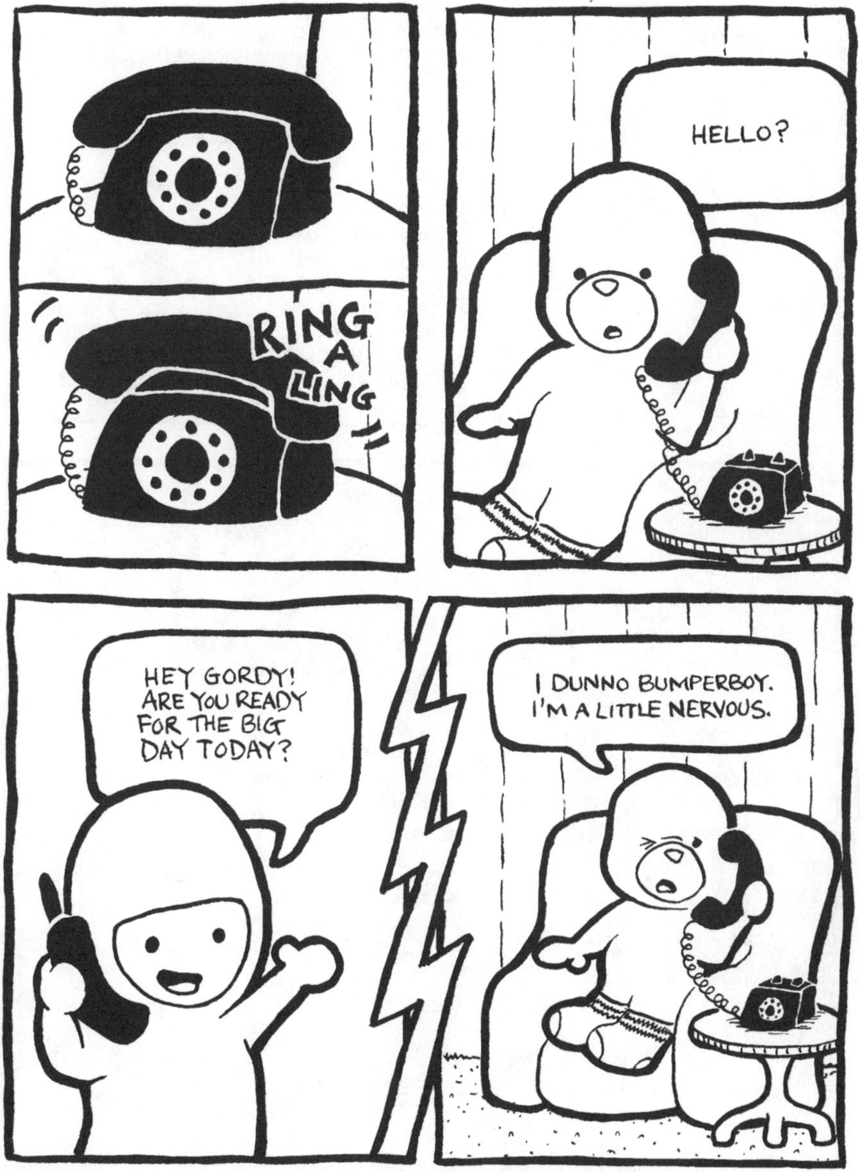
RING A LING
HELLO?
HEY GORDY! ARE YOU READY FOR THE BIG DAY TODAY?
I DUNNO BUMPERBOY. I'M A LITTLE NERVOUS.

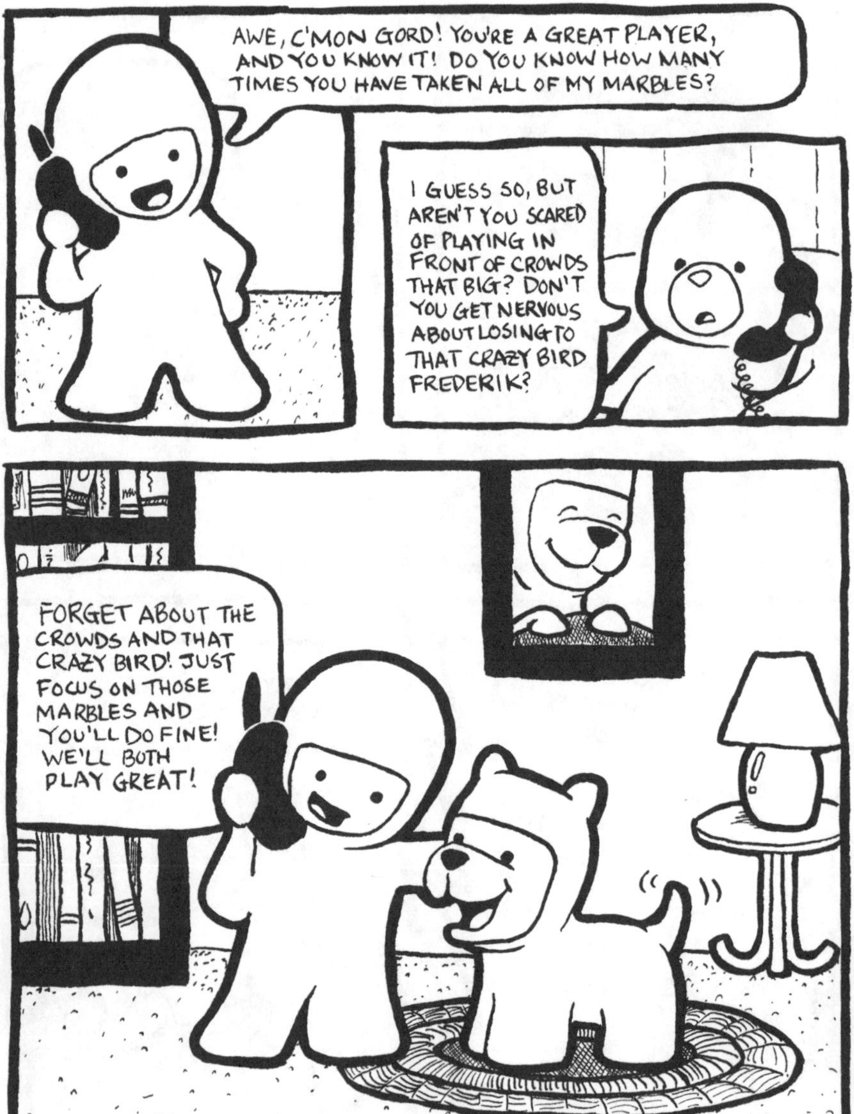
AWE, C'MON GORD! YOU'RE A GREAT PLAYER, AND YOU KNOW IT! DO YOU KNOW HOW MANY TIMES YOU HAVE TAKEN ALL OF MY MARBLES?
I GUESS SO, BUT AREN'T YOU SCARED OF PLAYING IN FRONT OF CROWDS THAT BIG? DON'T YOU GET NERVOUS ABOUT LOSING TO THAT CRAZY BIRD FREDERIK?
FORGET ABOUT THE CROWDS AND THAT CRAZY BIRD! JUST FOCUS ON THOSE MARBLES AND YOU'LL DO FINE! WE'LL BOTH PLAY GREAT!

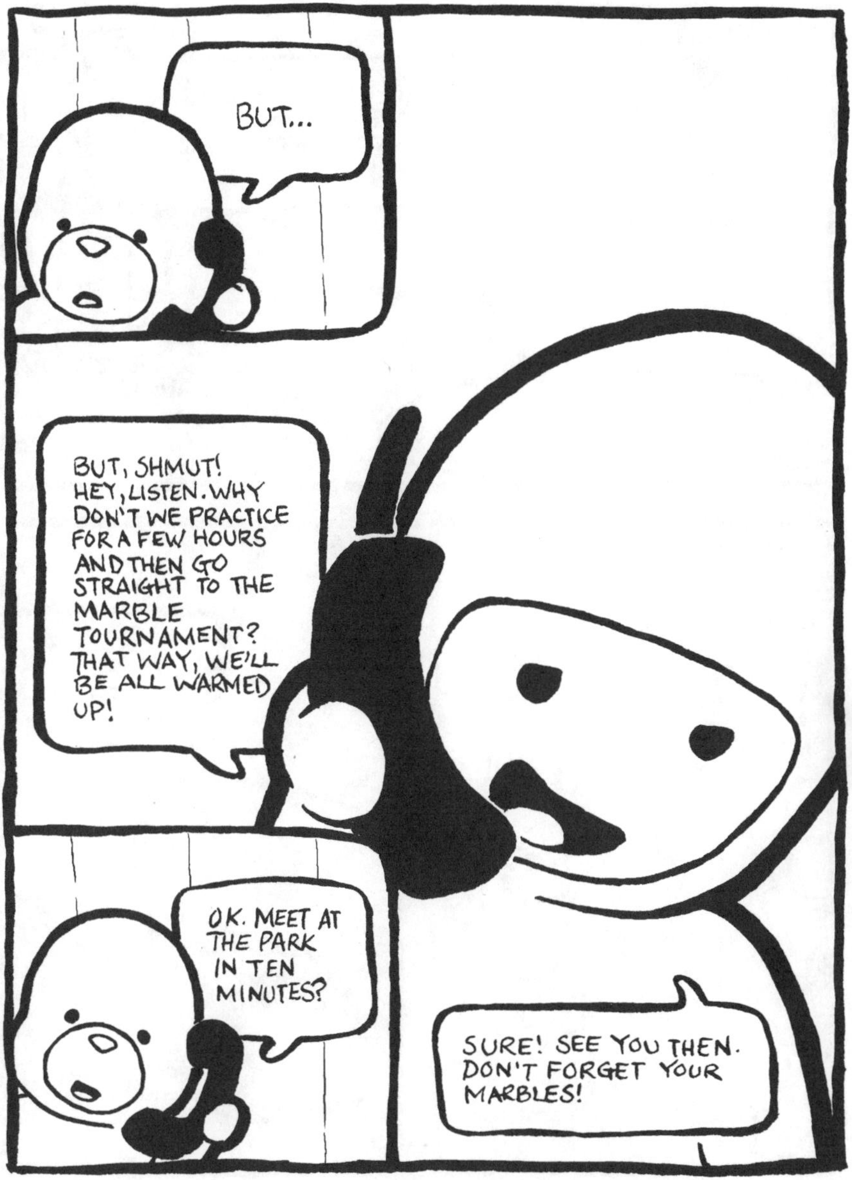
BUT...
BUT, SHMUT! HEY, LISTEN. WHY DON'T WE PRACTICE FOR A FEW HOURS AND THEN GO STRAIGHT TO THE MARBLE TOURNAMENT? THAT WAY, WE'LL BE ALL WARMED UP!
OK. MEET AT THE PARK IN TEN MINUTES?
SURE! SEE YOU THEN. DON'T FORGET YOUR MARBLES!

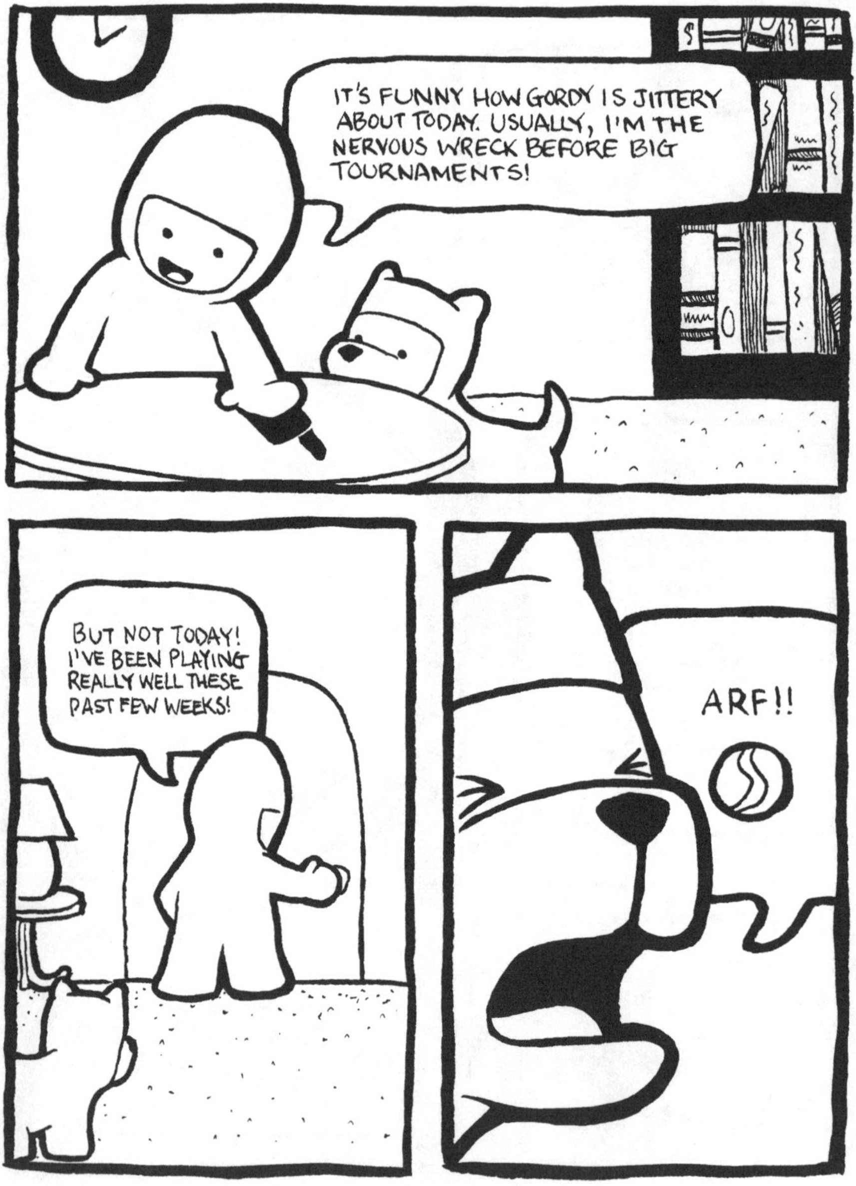
IT'S FUNNY HOW GORDY IS JITTERY ABOUT TODAY. USUALLY, I'M THE NERVOUS WRECK BEFORE BIG TOURNAMENTS!
BUT NOT TODAY! I'VE BEEN PLAYING REALLY WELL THESE PAST FEW WEEKS!
ARF!!

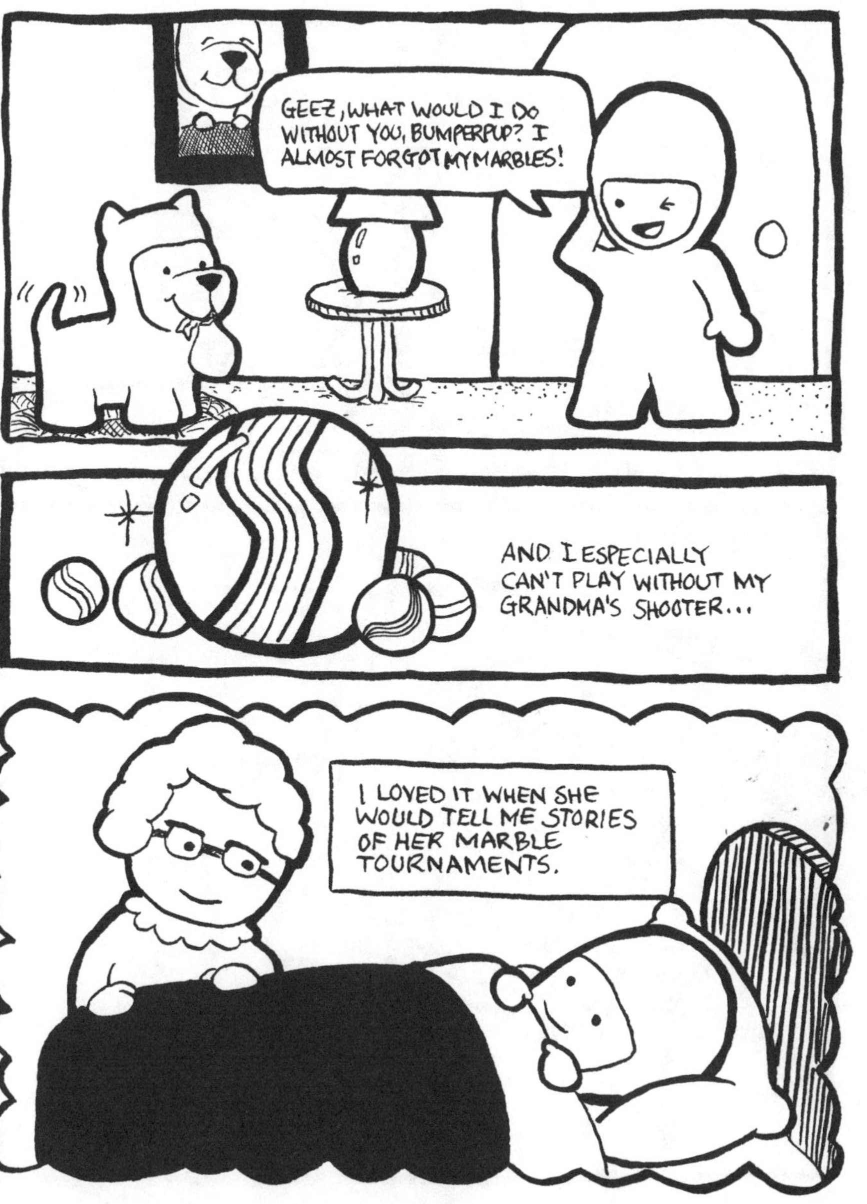
GEEZ, WHAT WOULD I DO WITHOUT YOU, BUMPERPUP? I ALMOST FORGOT MY MARBLES!
AND I ESPECIALLY CAN'T PLAY WITHOUT MY GRANDMA'S SHOOTER...
I LOVED IT WHEN SHE WOULD TELL ME STORIES OF HER MARBLE TOURNAMENTS.

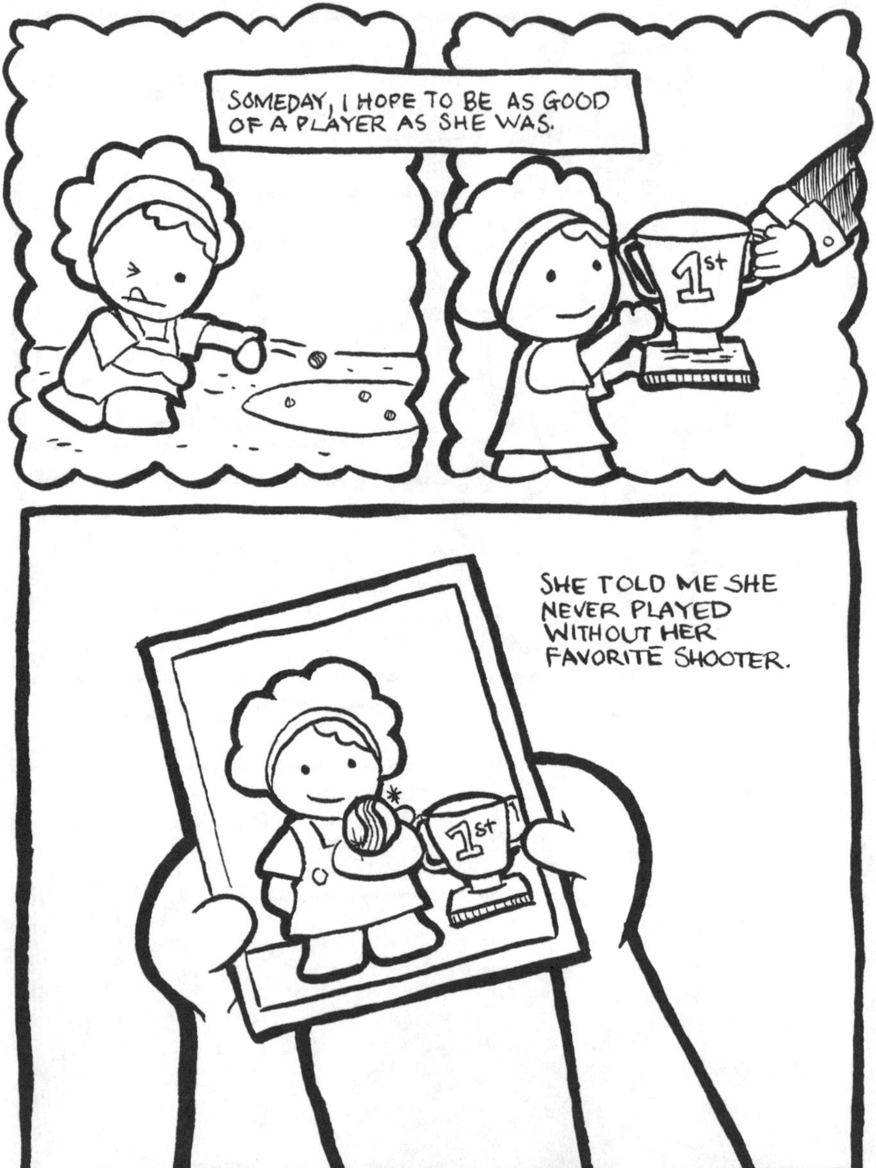
SOMEDAY, I HOPE TO BE AS GOOD OF A PLAYER AS SHE WAS.
1st
SHE TOLD ME SHE NEVER PLAYED WITHOUT HER FAVORITE SHOOTER.
1st

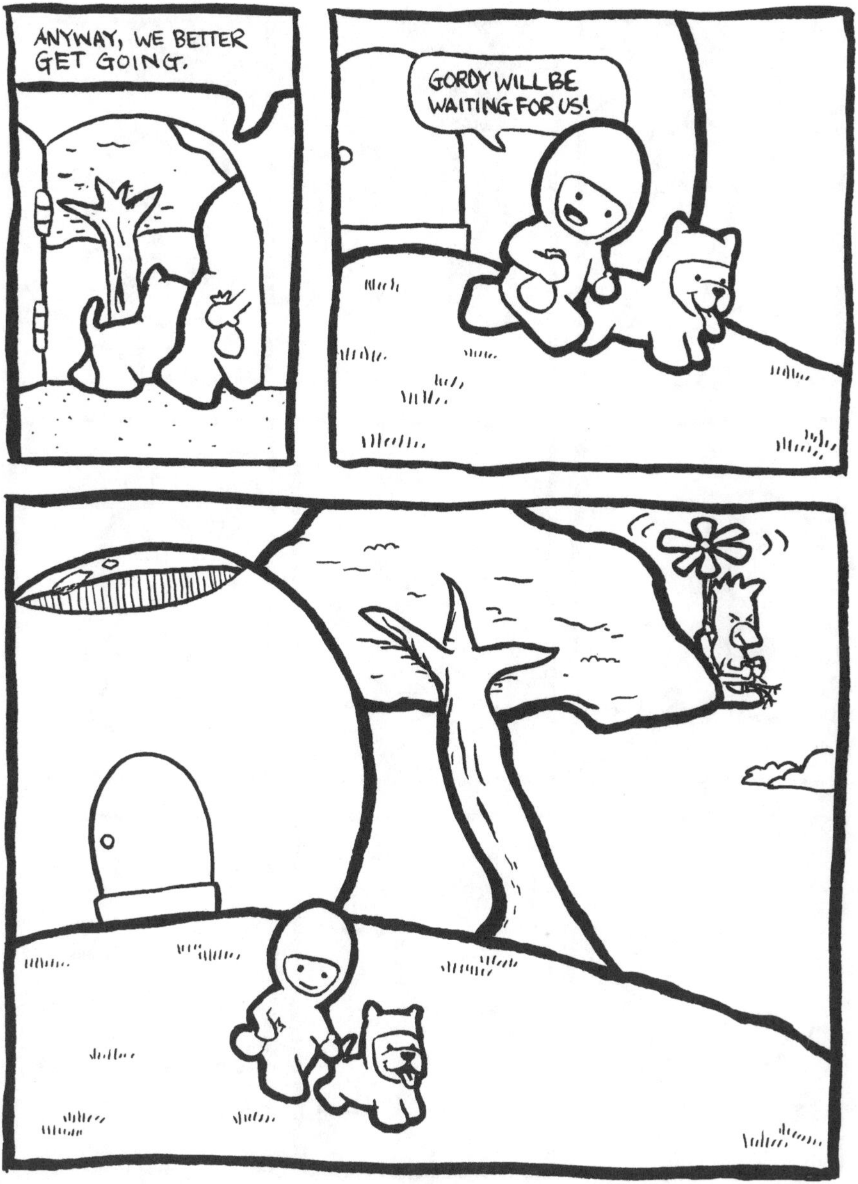
ANYWAY, WE BETTER GET GOING.
GORDY WILL BE WAITING FOR US!

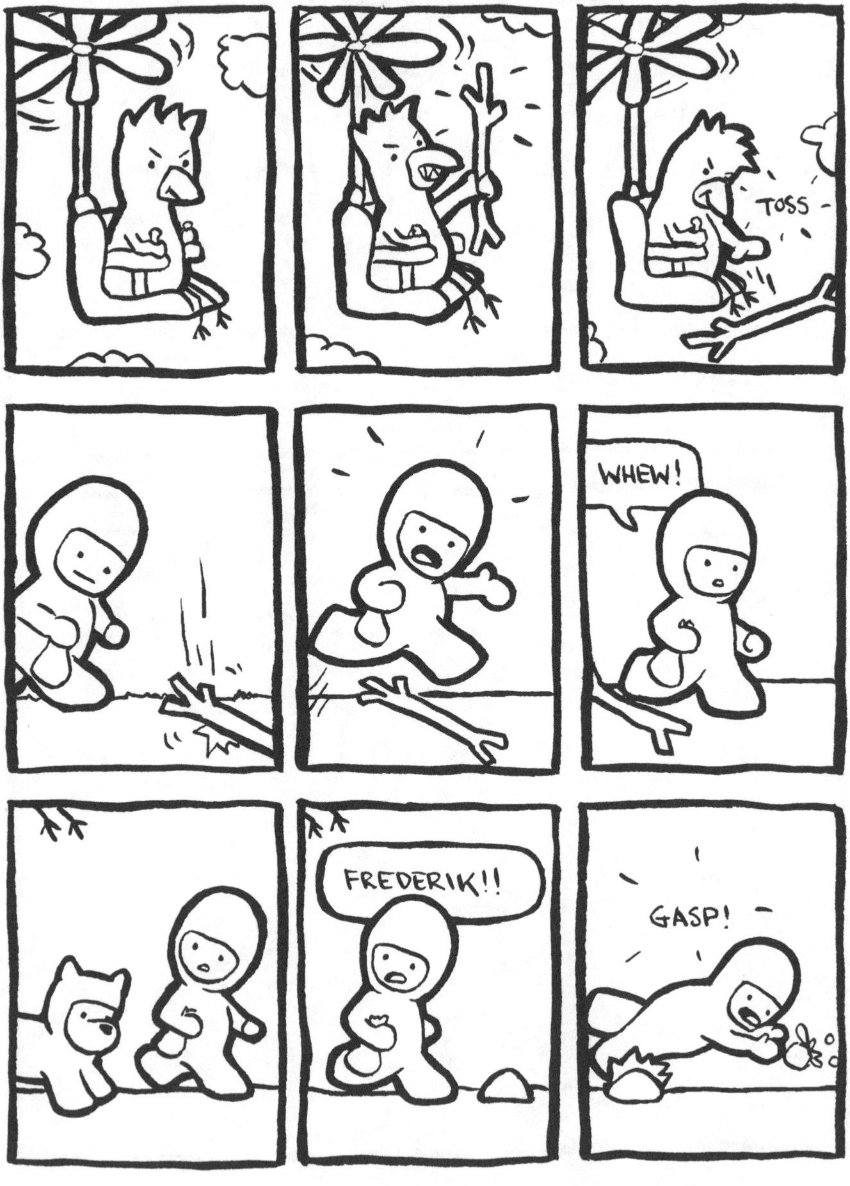
TOSS
WHEW!
FREDERIK!!
GASP!

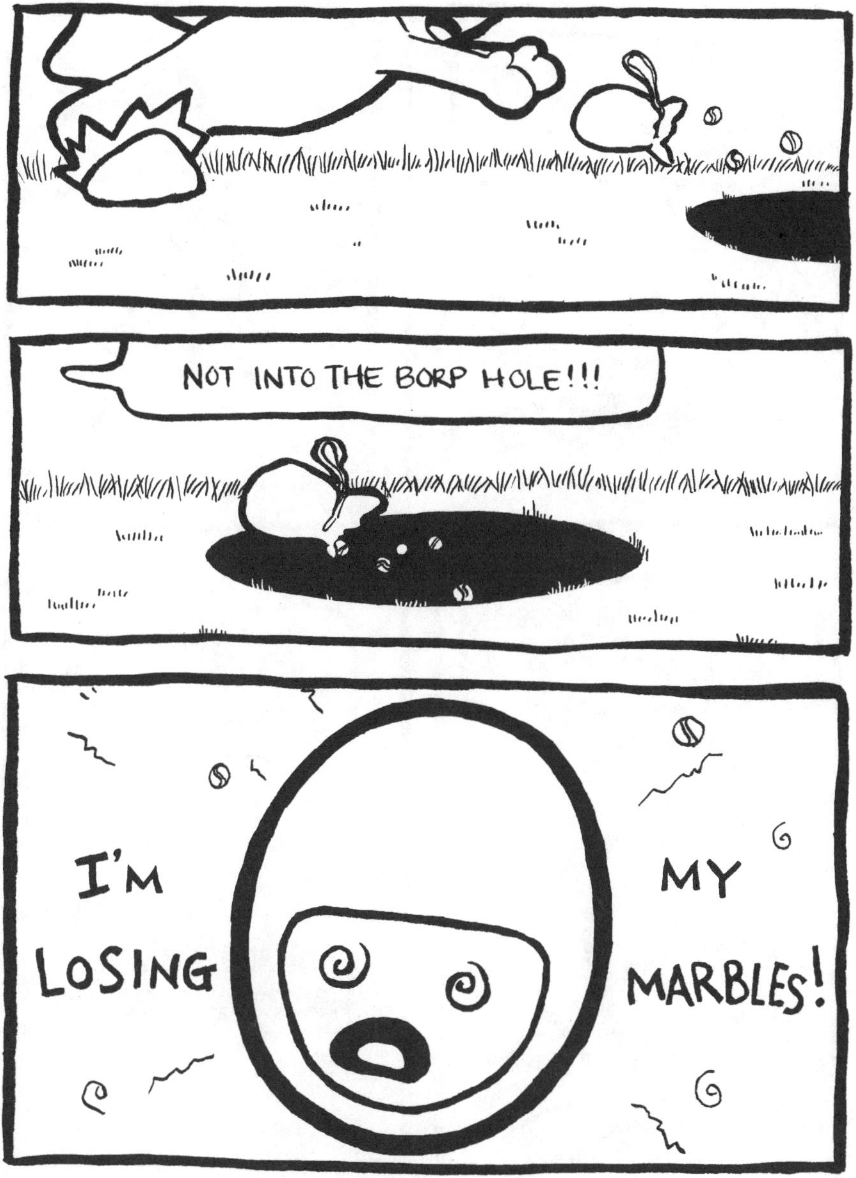
NOT INTO THE BORP HOLE!!!
I'M LOSING MY MARBLES!

THOSE MARBLES CAN END UP ANYWHERE! WHAT ARE WE GOING TO DO, BUMPERPUP??
ARF!
YOU'RE RIGHT, BUMPERPUP, I CAN'T PLAY IN THE TOURNAMENT WITHOUT MY MARBLES—ESPECIALLY GRANDMA'S SHOOTER!
WE'RE GOING TO HAVE TO SEARCH AS MANY DIFFERENT LANDS AS WE CAN.

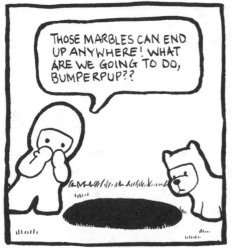

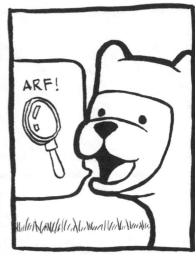

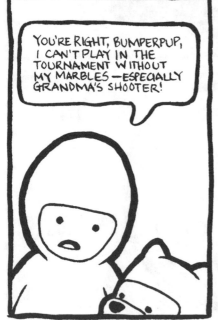

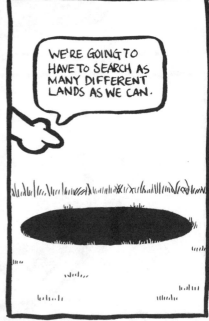

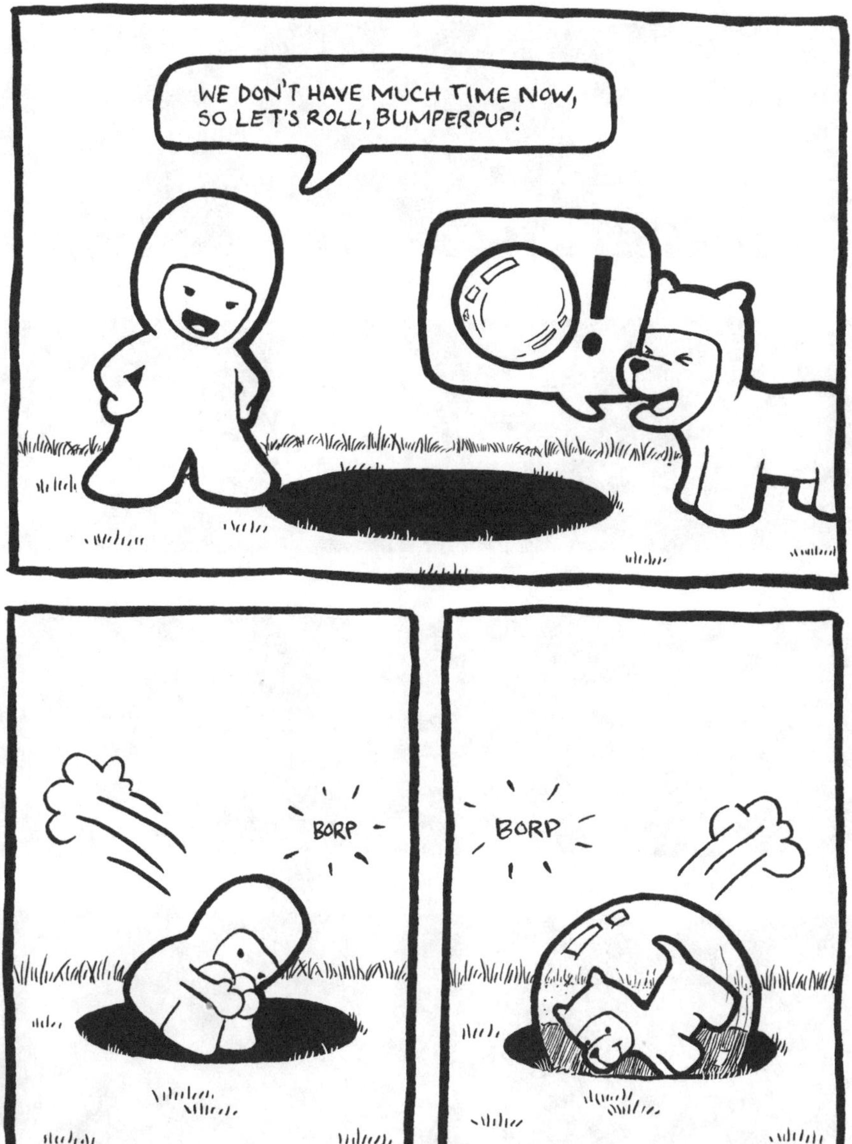
WE DON'T HAVE MUCH TIME NOW, SO LET'S ROLL, BUMPERPUP!
!
BORP
BORP

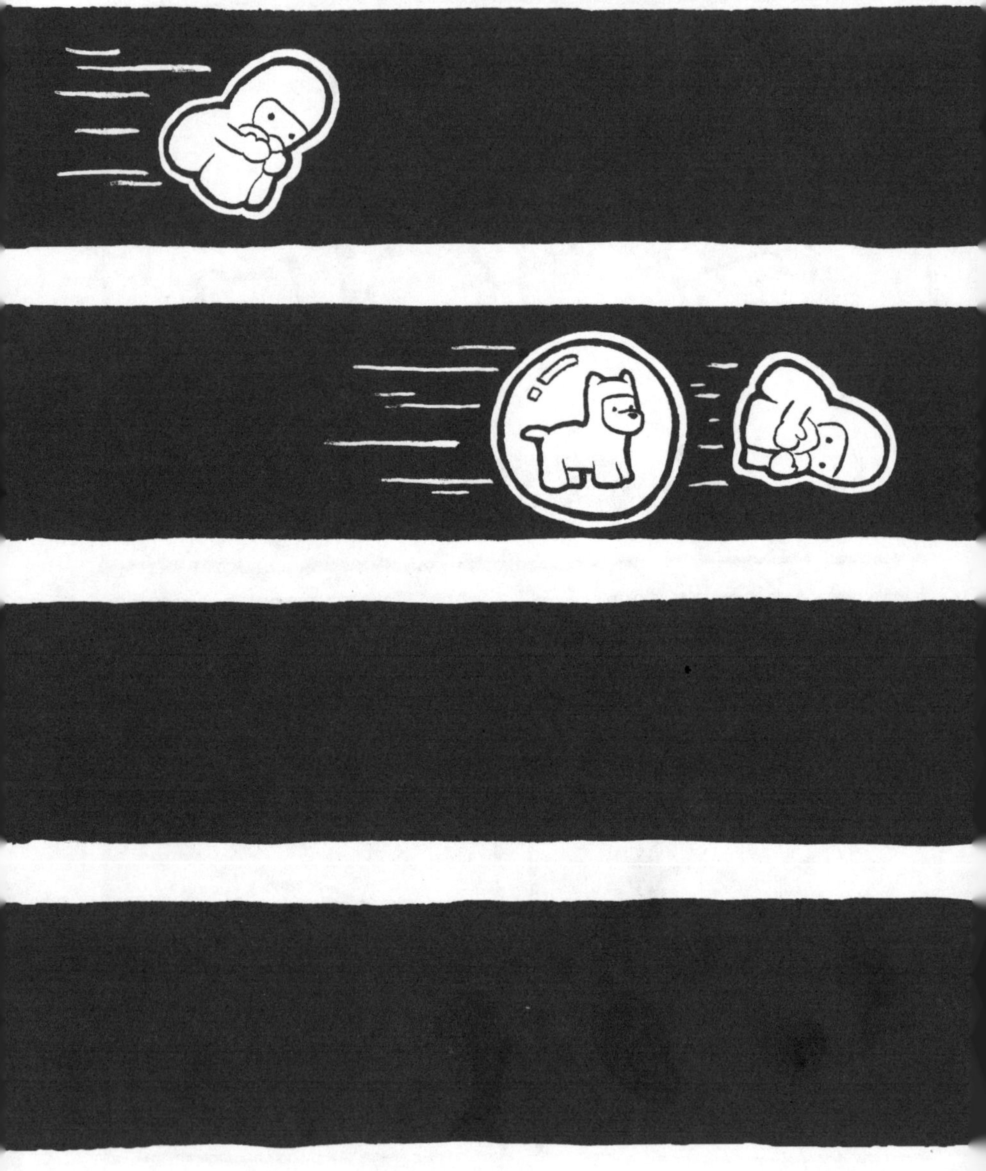

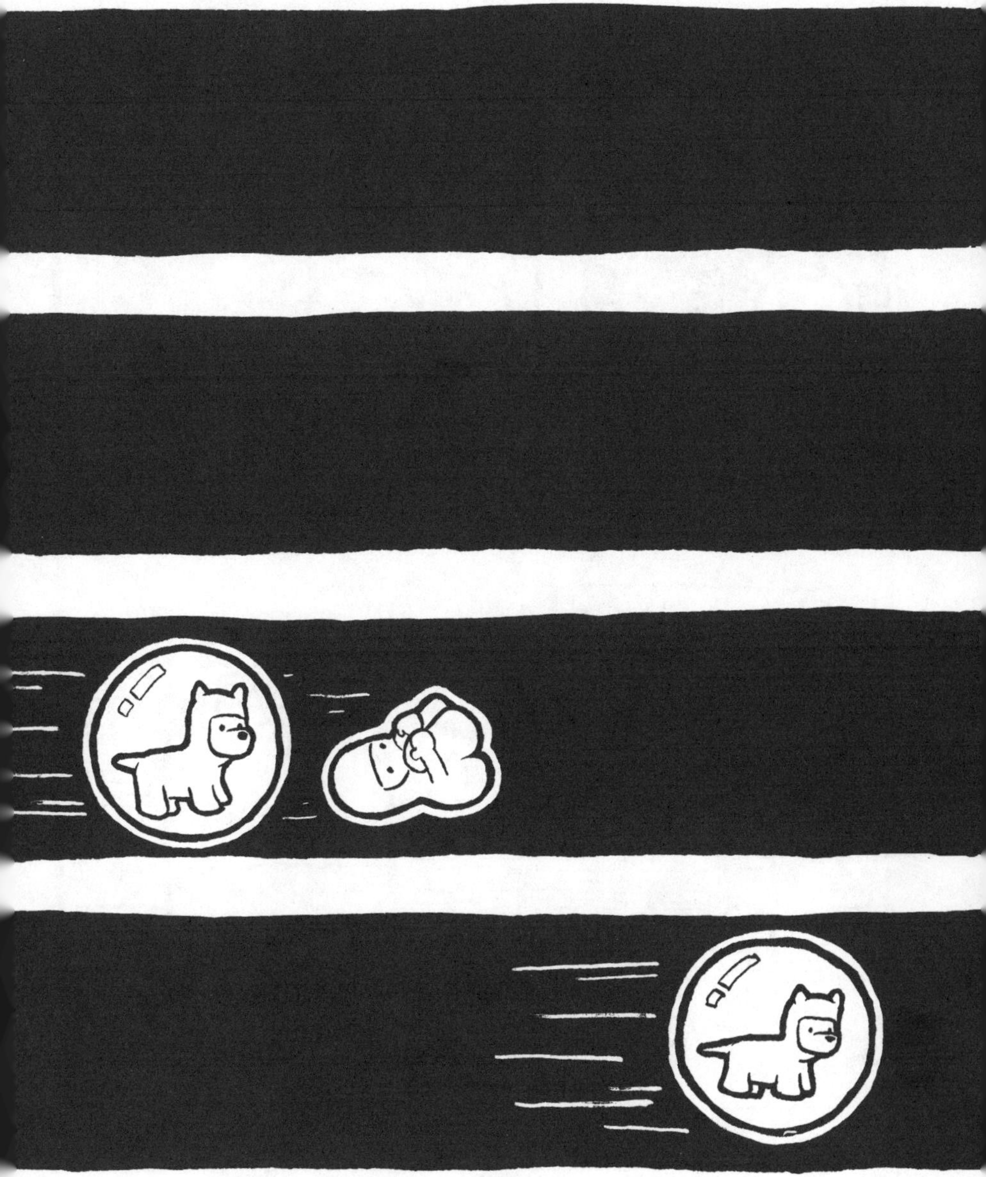

LET'S TRY THIS ONE...
WHERE ARE WE???
MEANWHILE...
PARK

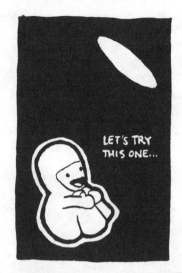

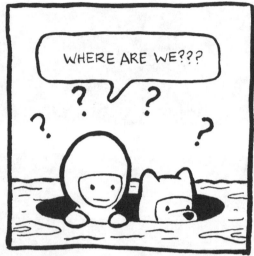

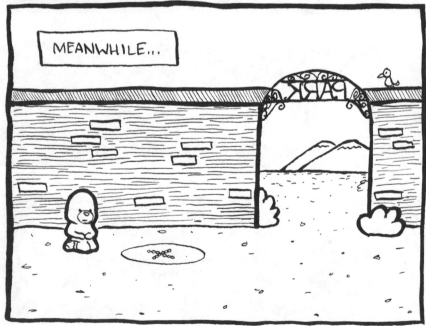

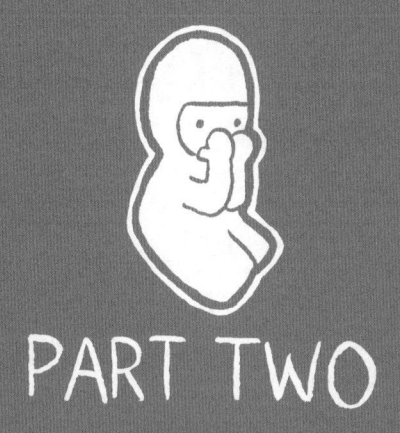

PART TWO

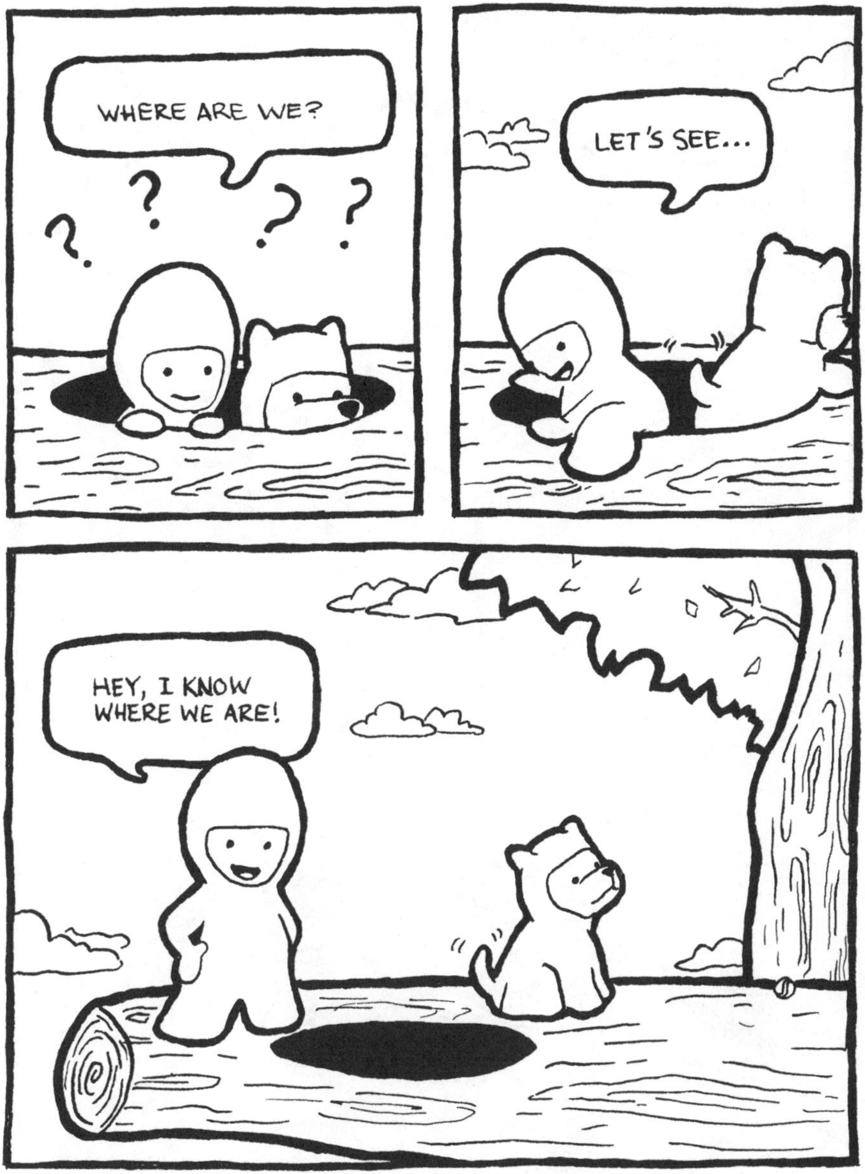
WHERE ARE WE?
? ? ? ?
LET'S SEE...
HEY, I KNOW WHERE WE ARE!

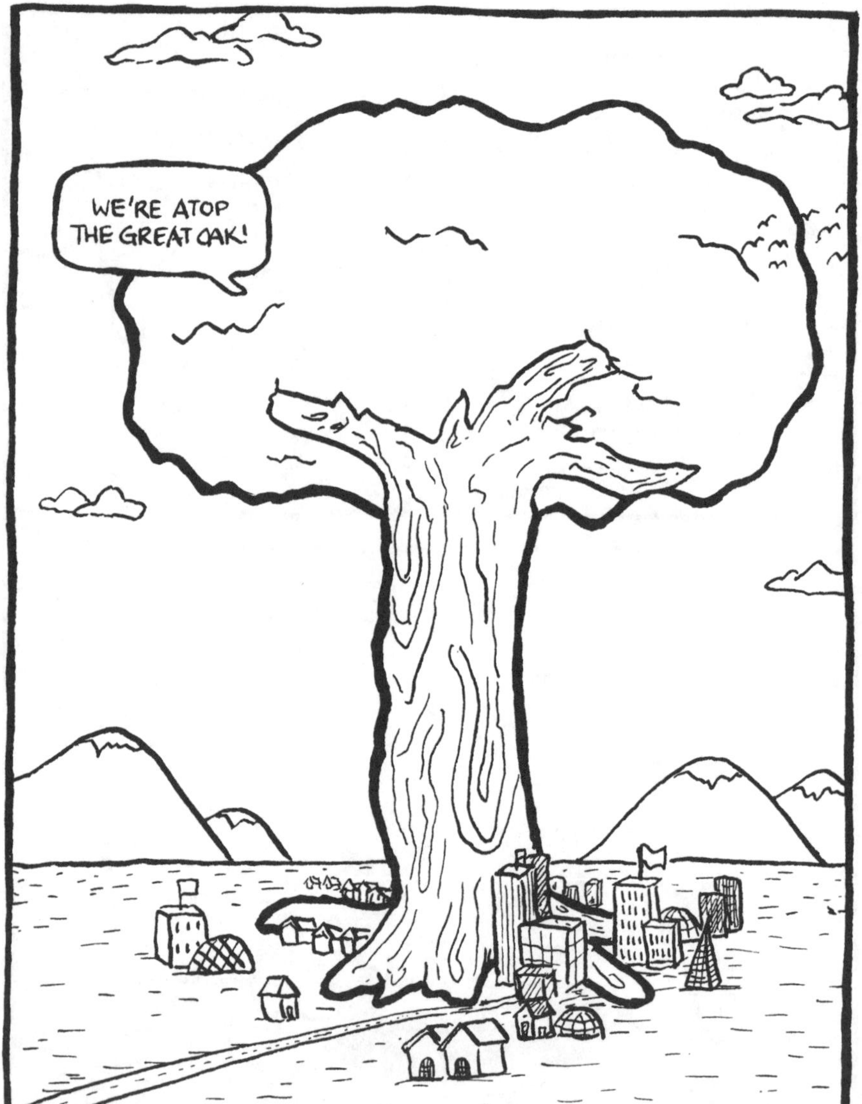
WE'RE ATOP THE GREAT OAK!

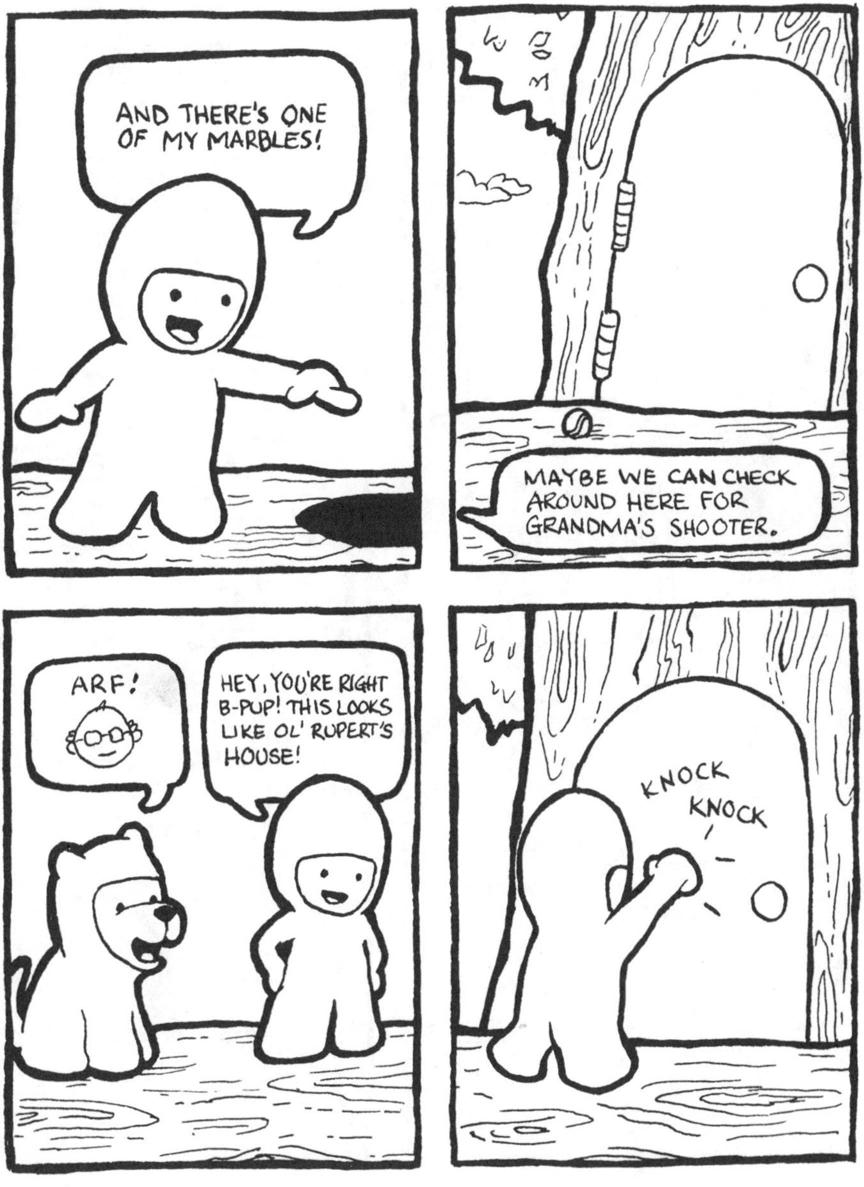
AND THERE'S ONE OF MY MARBLES!
MAYBE WE CAN CHECK AROUND HERE FOR GRANDMA'S SHOOTER.
ARF!
HEY, YOU'RE RIGHT B-PUP! THIS LOOKS LIKE OL' RUPERT'S HOUSE!
KNOCK
KNOCK

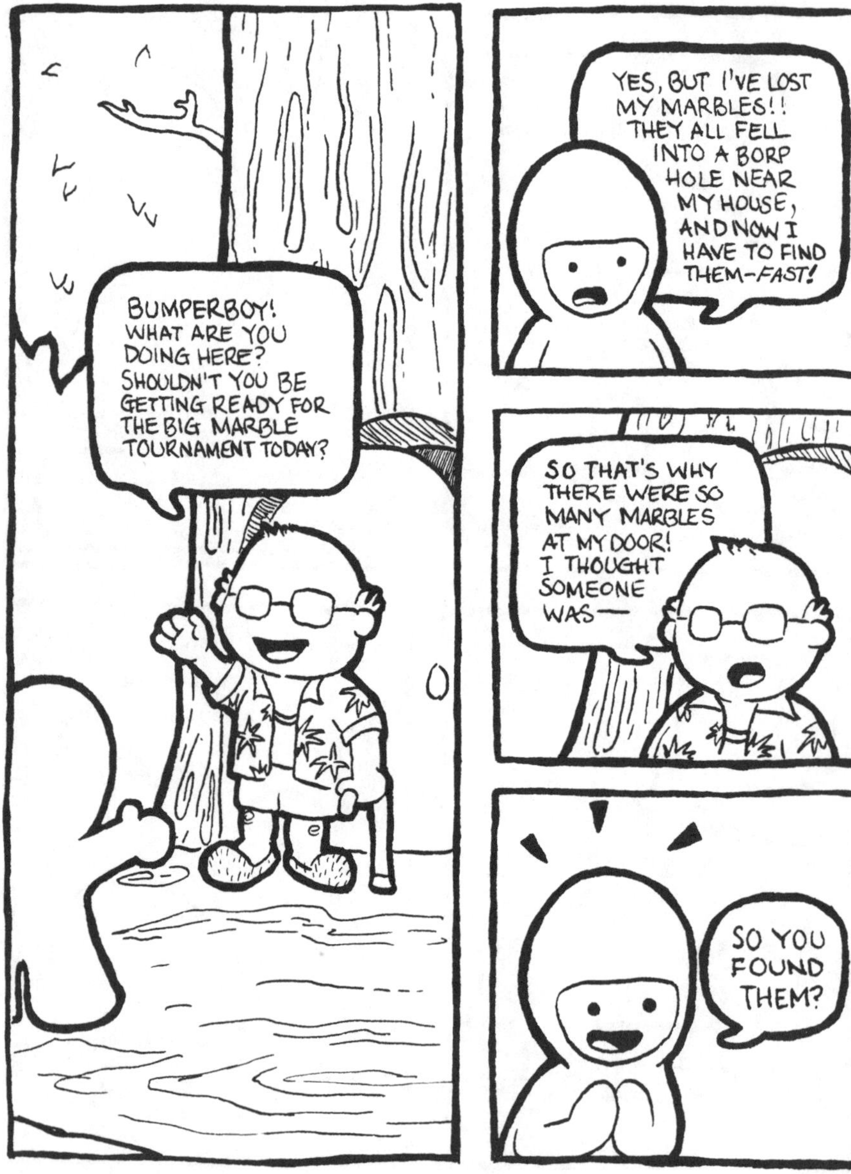
BUMPERBOY! WHAT ARE YOU DOING HERE? SHOULDN'T YOU BE GETTING READY FOR THE BIG MARBLE TOURNAMENT TODAY?
YES, BUT I'VE LOST MY MARBLES!! THEY ALL FELL INTO A BORP HOLE NEAR MY HOUSE, AND NOW I HAVE TO FIND THEM—FAST!
SO THAT'S WHY THERE WERE SO MANY MARBLES AT MY DOOR! I THOUGHT SOMEONE WAS—
SO YOU FOUND THEM?

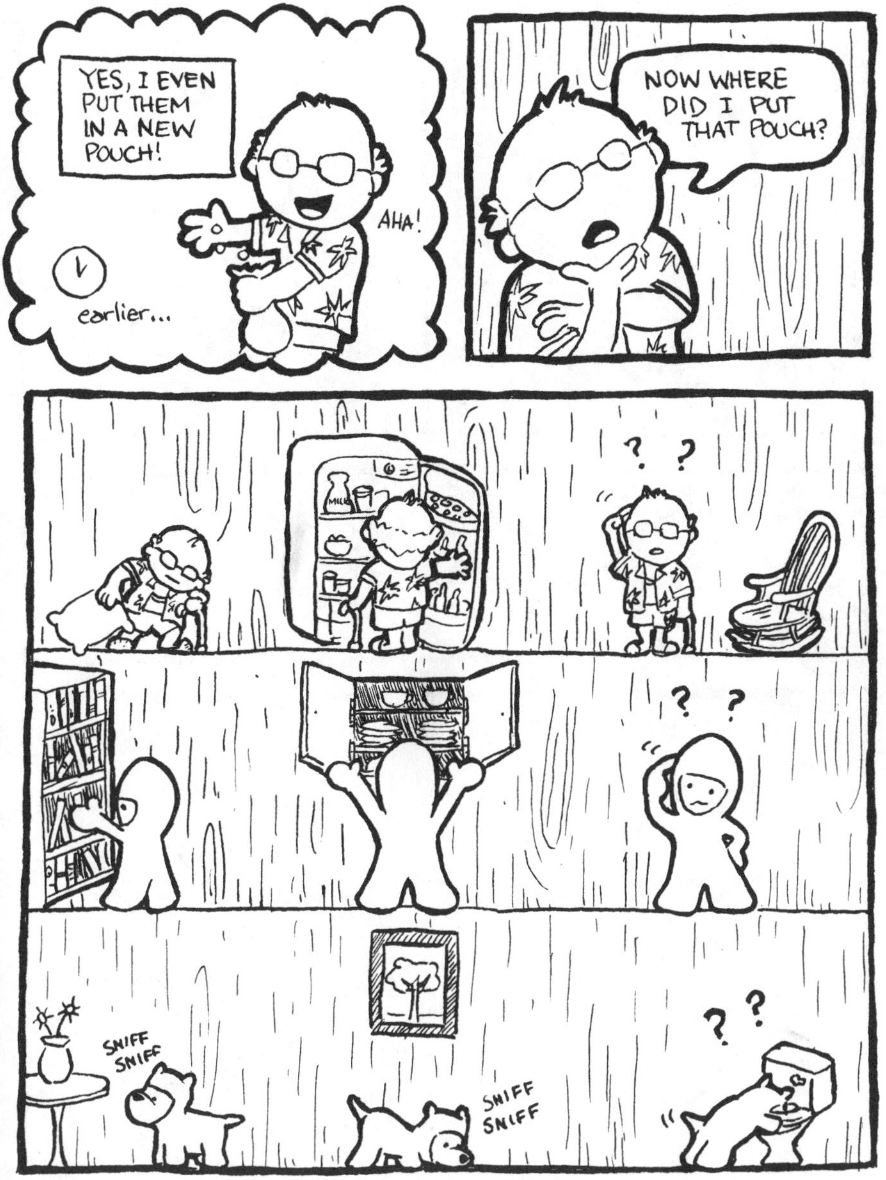
YES, I EVEN PUT THEM IN A NEW POUCH!
earlier...
AHA!
NOW WHERE DID I PUT THAT POUCH?
MILK
SNIFF SNIFF
SNIFF SNIFF

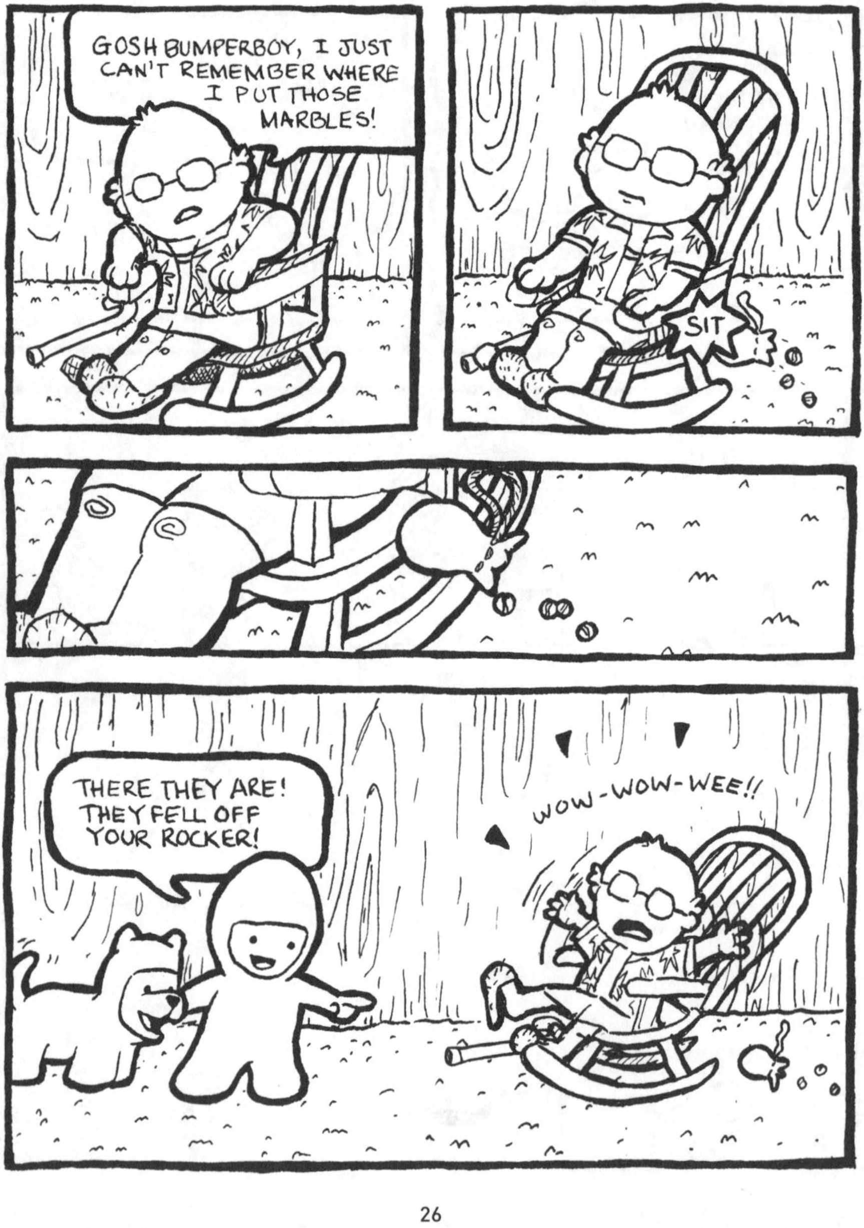
GOSH BUMPERBOY, I JUST CAN'T REMEMBER WHERE I PUT THOSE MARBLES!
SIT
THERE THEY ARE! THEY FELL OFF YOUR ROCKER!
WOW-WOW-WEE!!

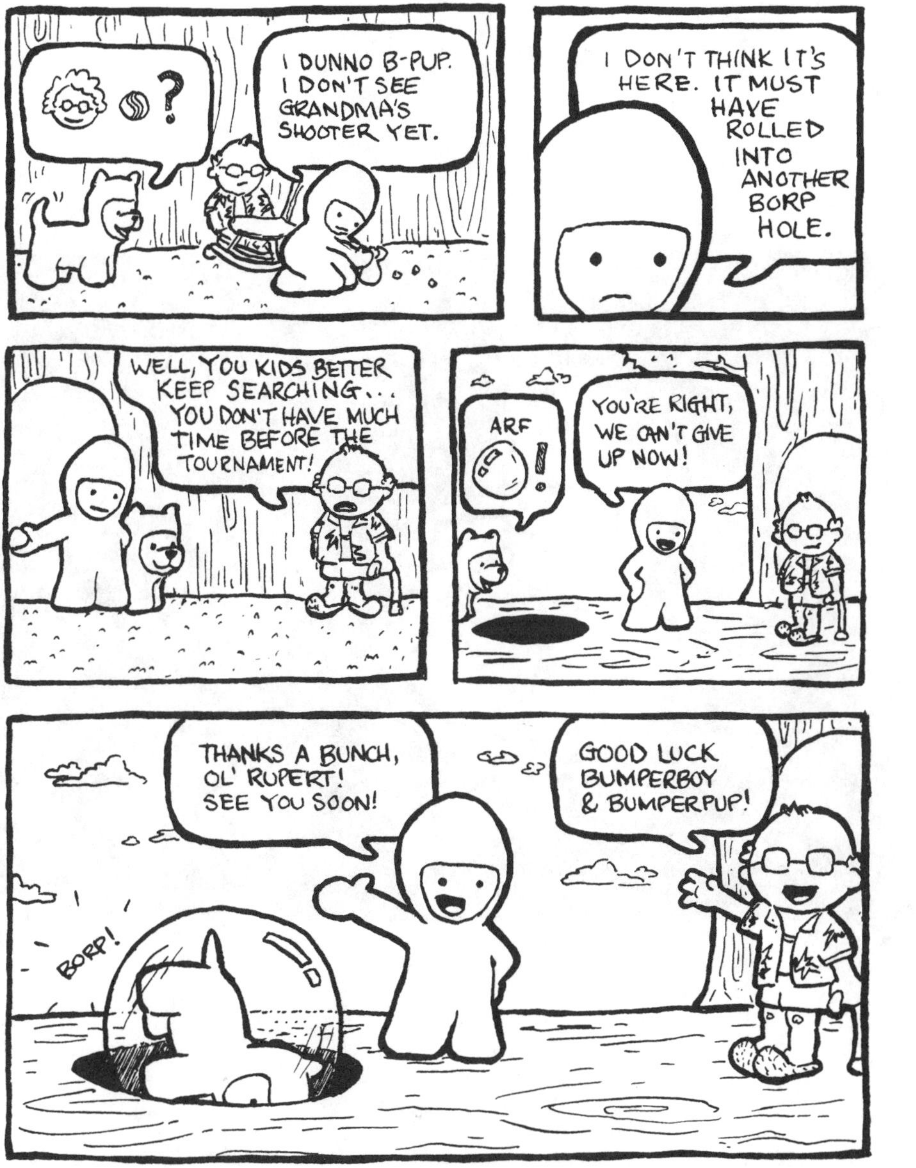
?
I DUNNO B-PUP. I DON'T SEE GRANDMA'S SHOOTER YET.
I DON'T THINK IT'S HERE. IT MUST HAVE ROLLED INTO ANOTHER BORP HOLE.
WELL, YOU KIDS BETTER KEEP SEARCHING... YOU DON'T HAVE MUCH TIME BEFORE THE TOURNAMENT!
ARF
!
YOU'RE RIGHT, WE CAN'T GIVE UP NOW!
THANKS A BUNCH, OL' RUPERT! SEE YOU SOON!
GOOD LUCK BUMPERBOY & BUMPERPUP!
BORP!

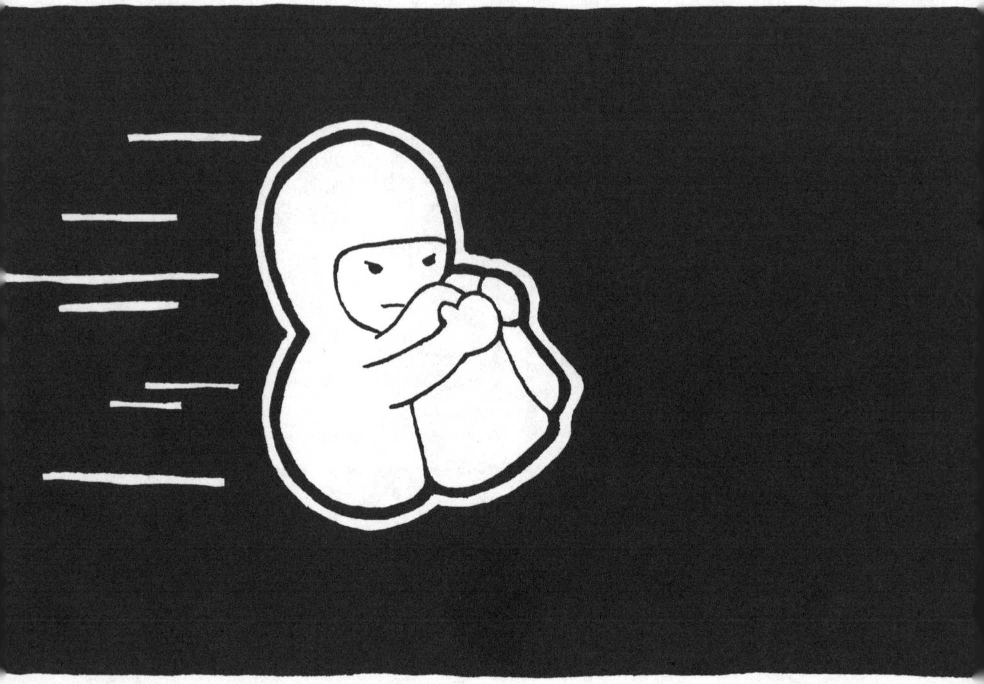

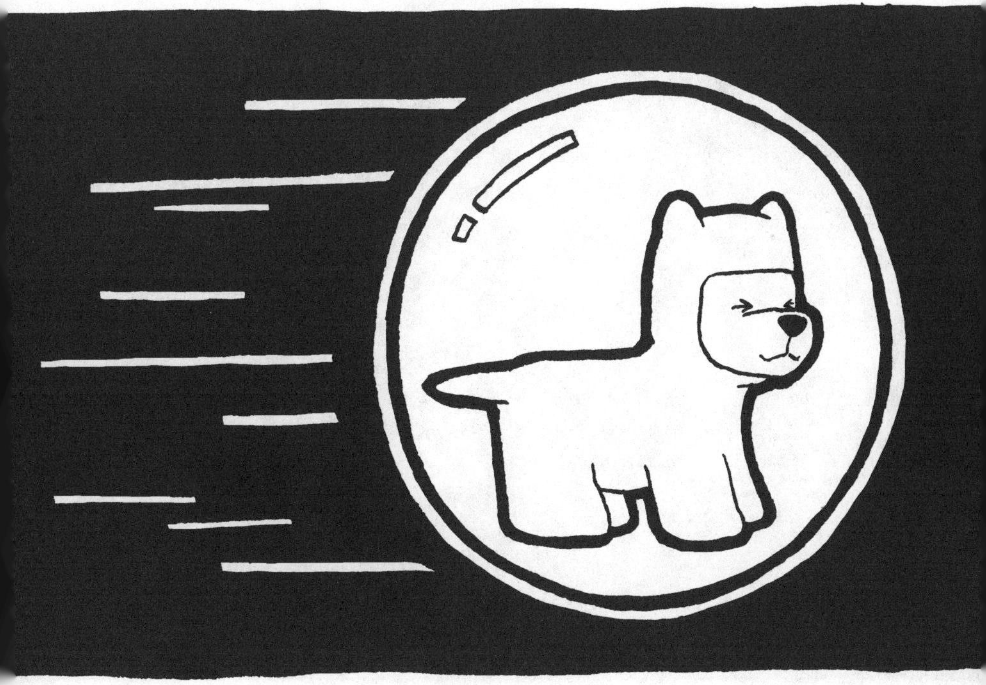

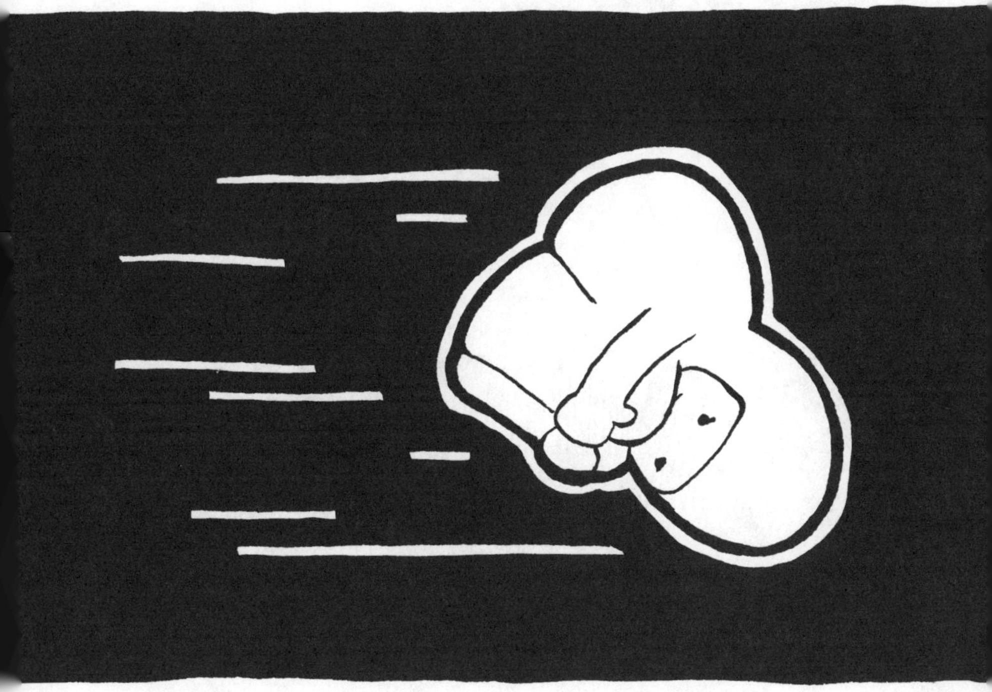

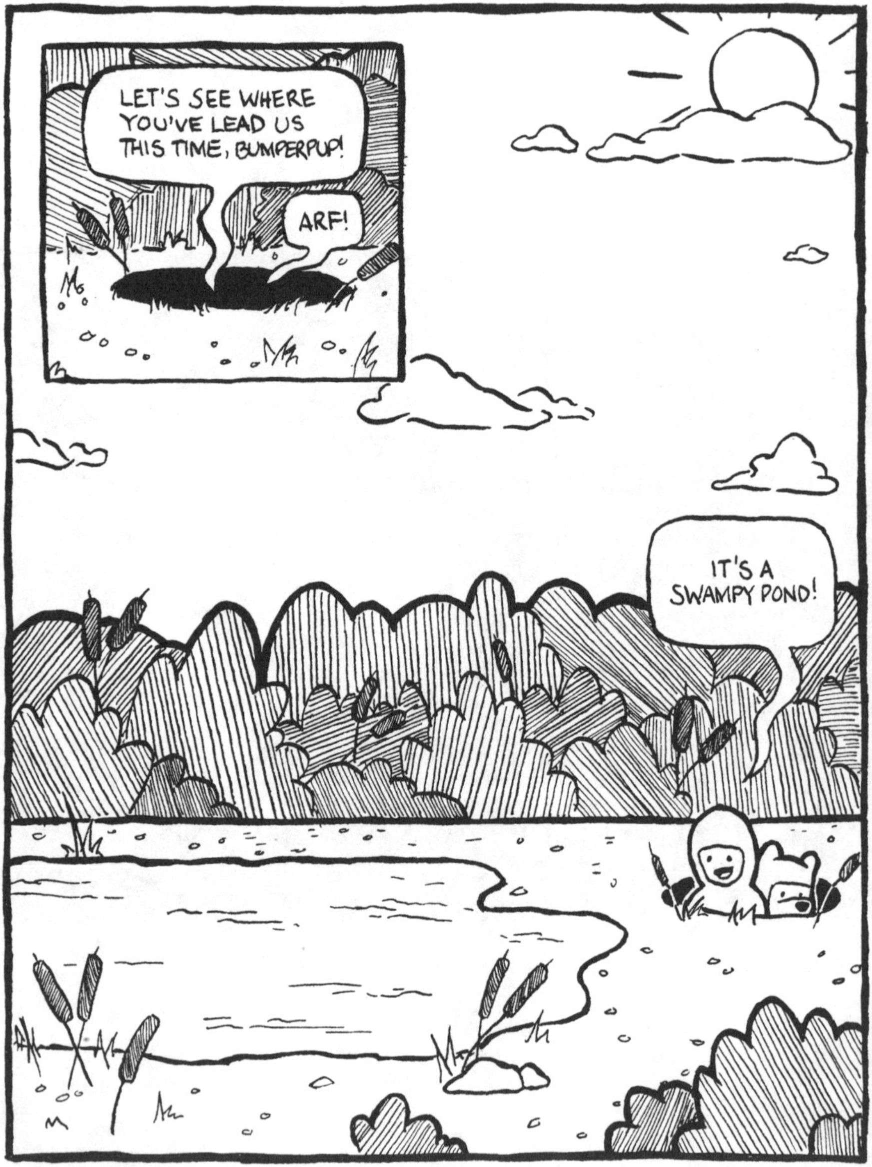
LET'S SEE WHERE YOU'VE LEAD US THIS TIME, BUMPERPUP!
ARF!
IT'S A SWAMPY POND!

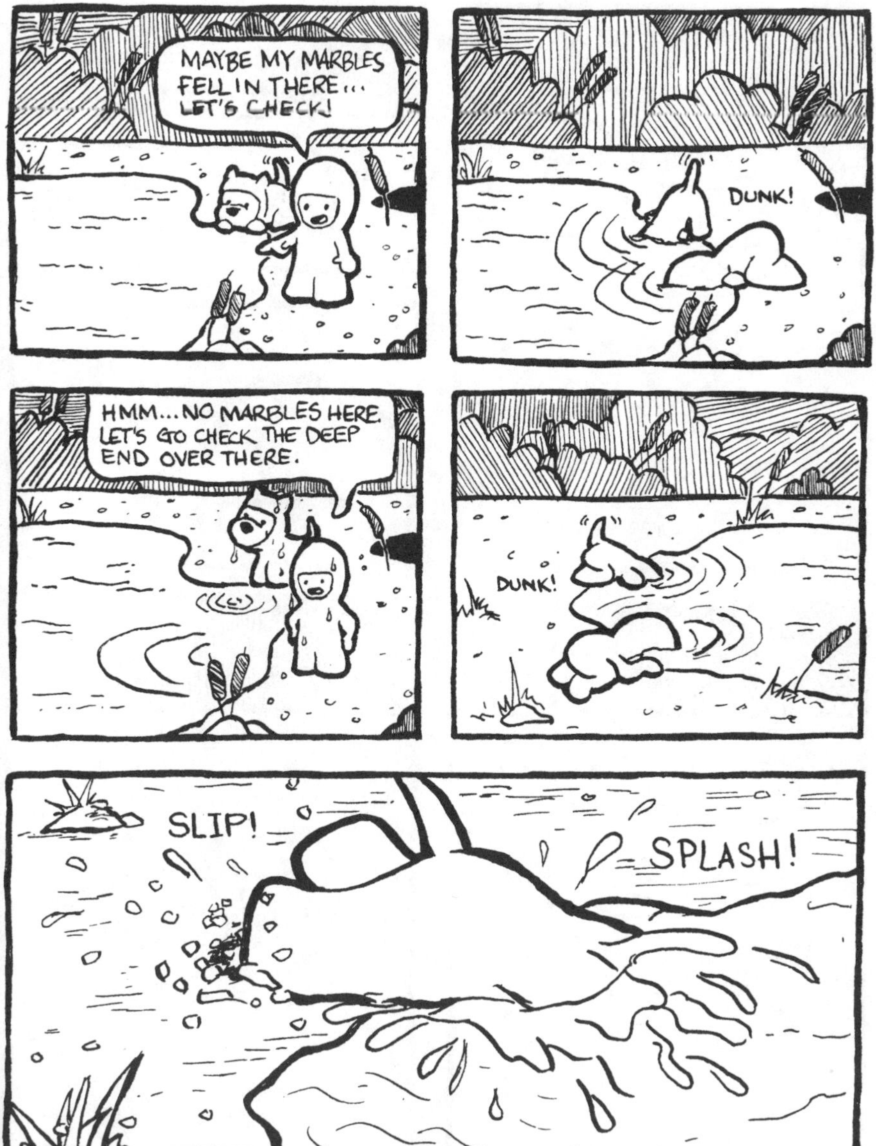
MAYBE MY MARBLES FELL IN THERE... LET'S CHECK!
DUNK!
HMM...NO MARBLES HERE. LET'S GO CHECK THE DEEP END OVER THERE.
DUNK!
SLIP!
SPLASH!

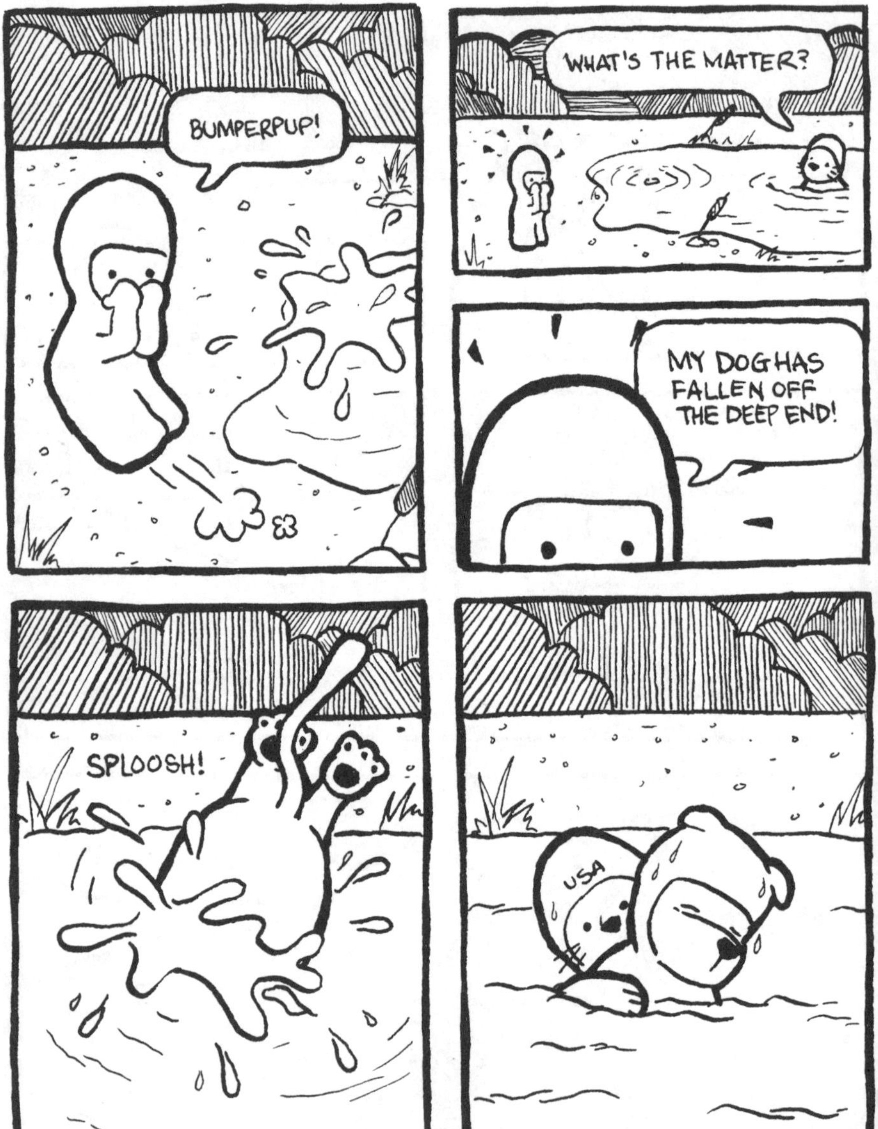
BUMPERPUP!
WHAT'S THE MATTER?
MY DOG HAS FALLEN OFF THE DEEP END!
SPLOOSH!
USA

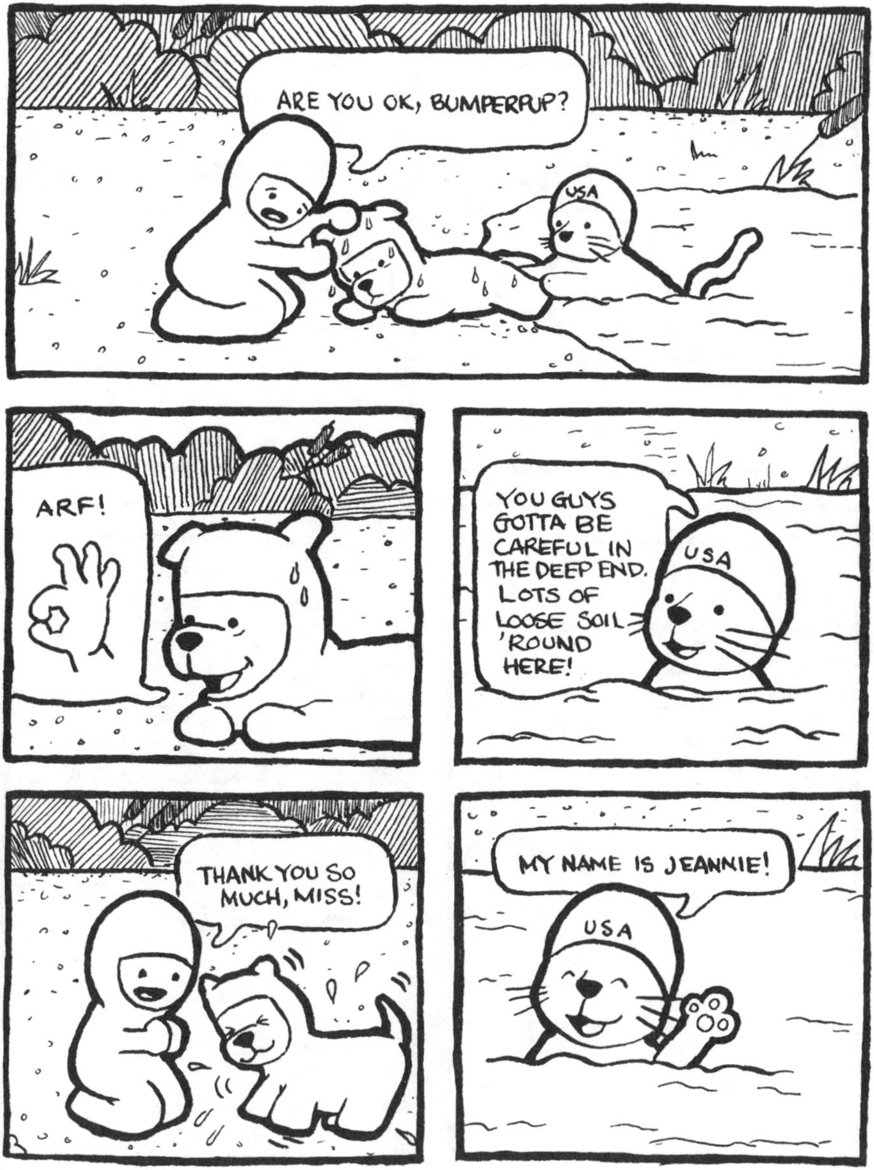
ARE YOU OK, BUMPERPUP?
ARF!
YOU GUYS GOTTA BE CAREFUL IN THE DEEP END. LOTS OF LOOSE SOIL 'ROUND HERE!
USA
THANK YOU SO MUCH, MISS!
MY NAME IS JEANNIE!
USA

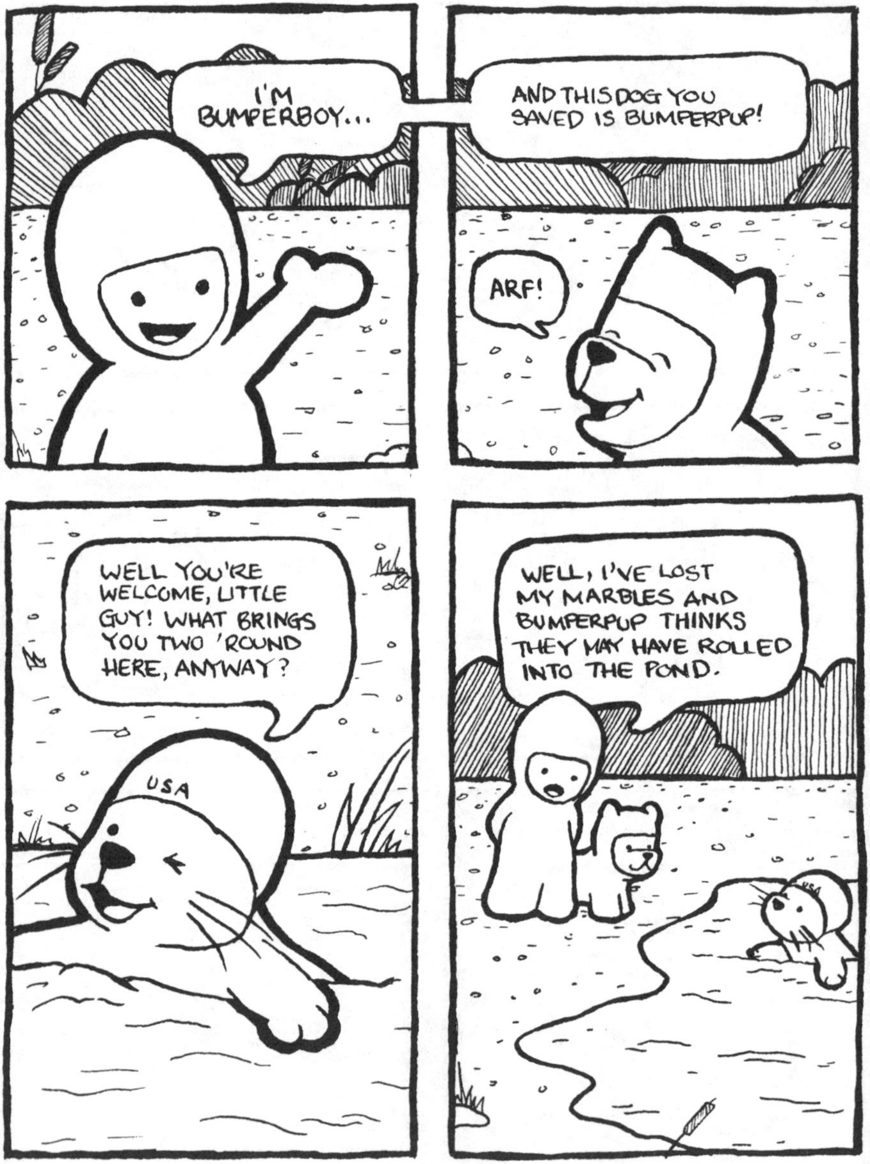
I'M BUMPERBOY...
AND THIS DOG YOU SAVED IS BUMPERPUP!
ARF!
USA
WELL YOU'RE WELCOME, LITTLE GUY! WHAT BRINGS YOU TWO 'ROUND HERE, ANYWAY?
WELL, I'VE LOST MY MARBLES AND BUMPERPUP THINKS THEY MAY HAVE ROLLED INTO THE POND.
USA

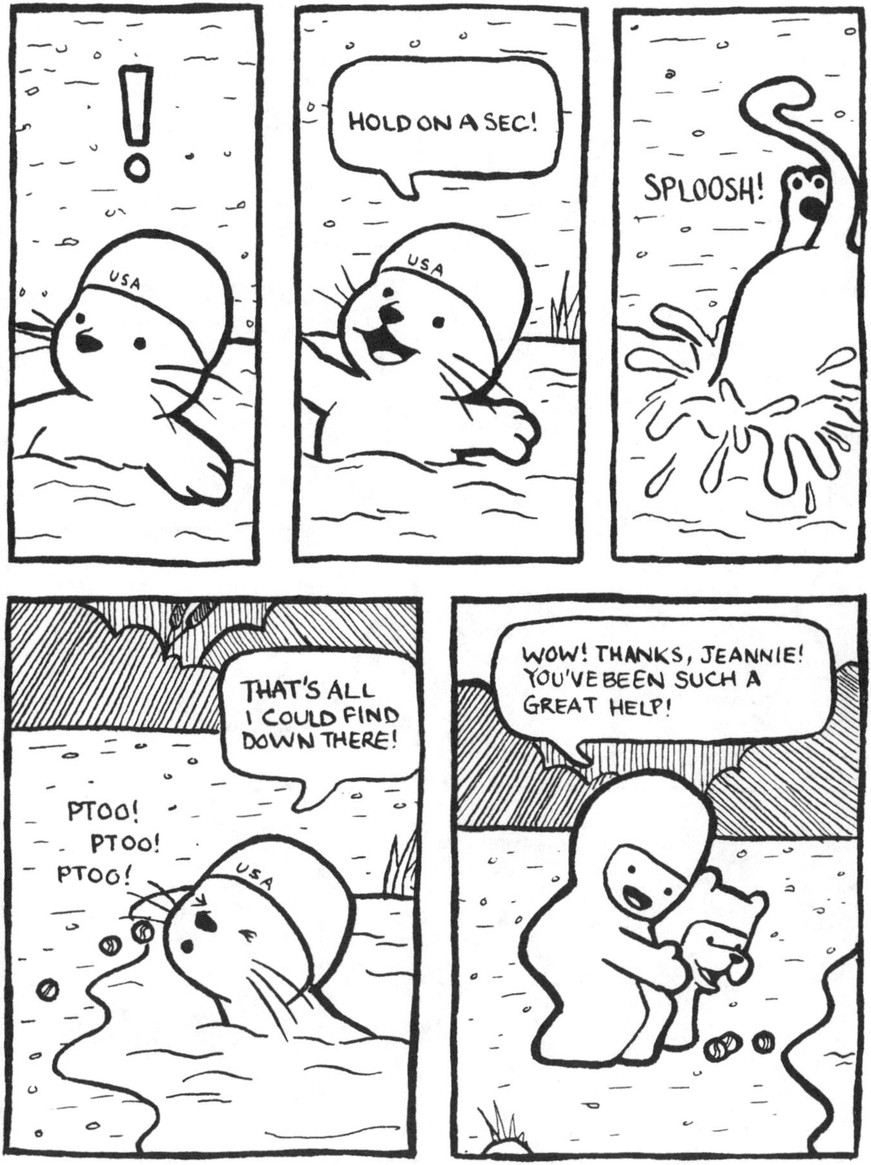
!
HOLD ON A SEC!
SPLOOSH!
THAT'S ALL I COULD FIND DOWN THERE!
PTOO! PTOO! PTOO!
USA
WOW! THANKS, JEANNIE! YOU'VE BEEN SUCH A GREAT HELP!

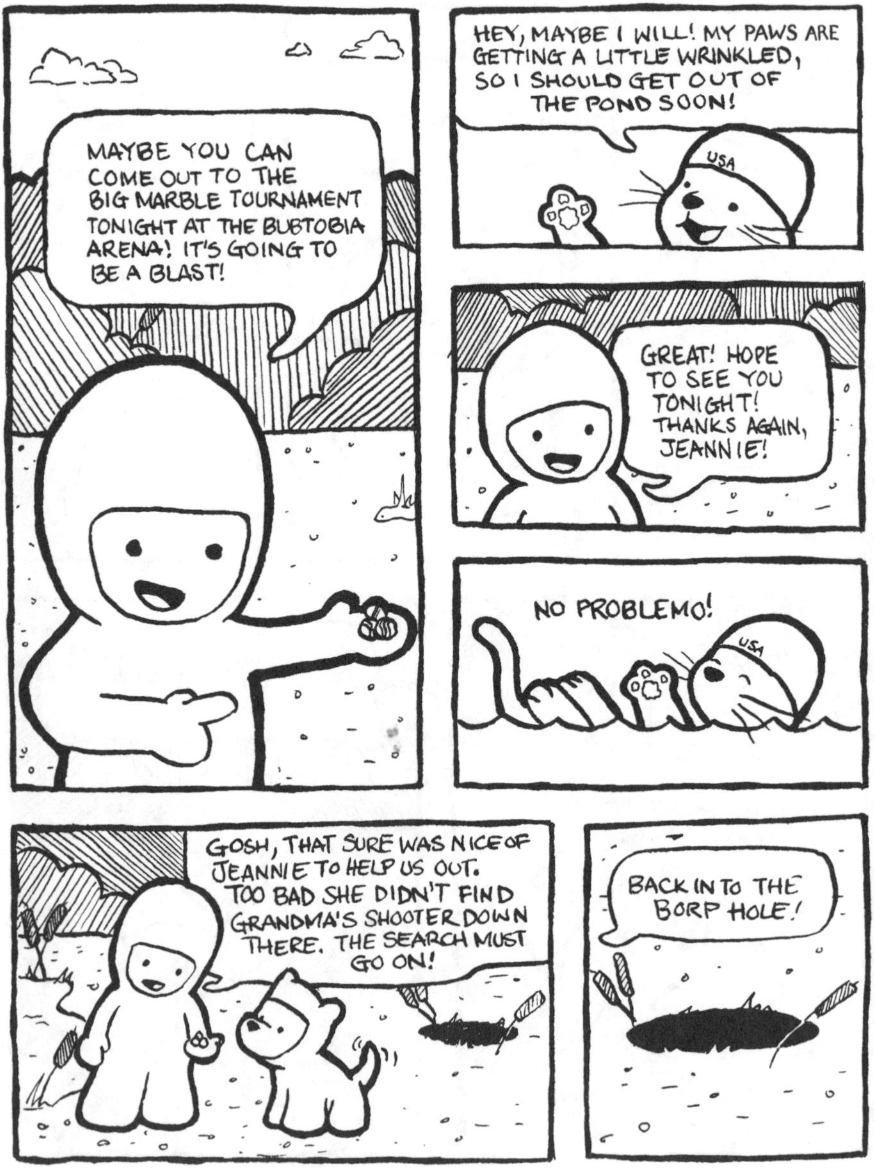
MAYBE YOU CAN COME OUT TO THE BIG MARBLE TOURNAMENT TONIGHT AT THE BUBTOBIA ARENA! IT'S GOING TO BE A BLAST!
HEY, MAYBE I WILL! MY PAWS ARE GETTING A LITTLE WRINKLED, SO I SHOULD GET OUT OF THE POND SOON!
USA
GREAT! HOPE TO SEE YOU TONIGHT! THANKS AGAIN, JEANNIE!
NO PROBLEMO!
USA
GOSH, THAT SURE WAS NICE OF JEANNIE TO HELP US OUT. TOO BAD SHE DIDN'T FIND GRANDMA'S SHOOTER DOWN THERE. THE SEARCH MUST GO ON!
BACK IN TO THE BORP HOLE!

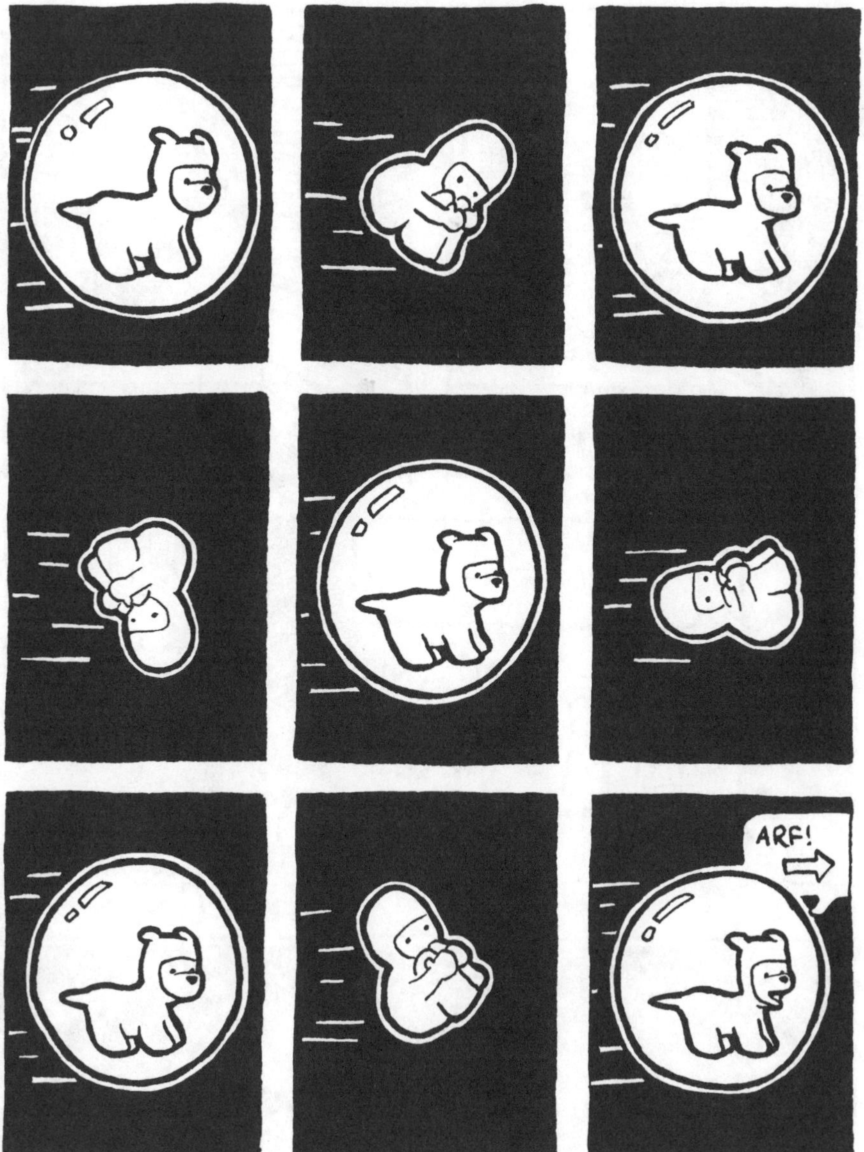
ARF!

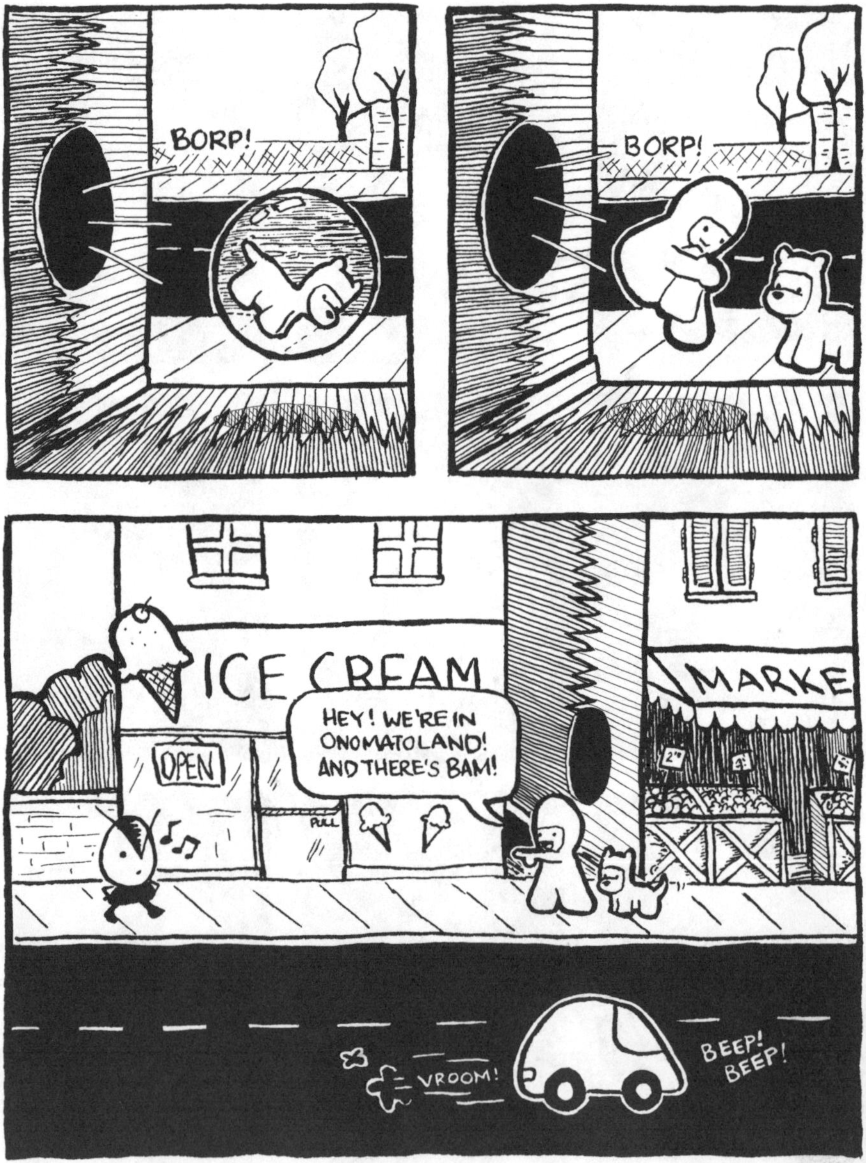
BORP!
BORP!
ICE CREAM
MARKE
OPEN
PULL
HEY! WE'RE IN ONOMATOLAND! AND THERE'S BAM!
VROOM!
BEEP! BEEP!

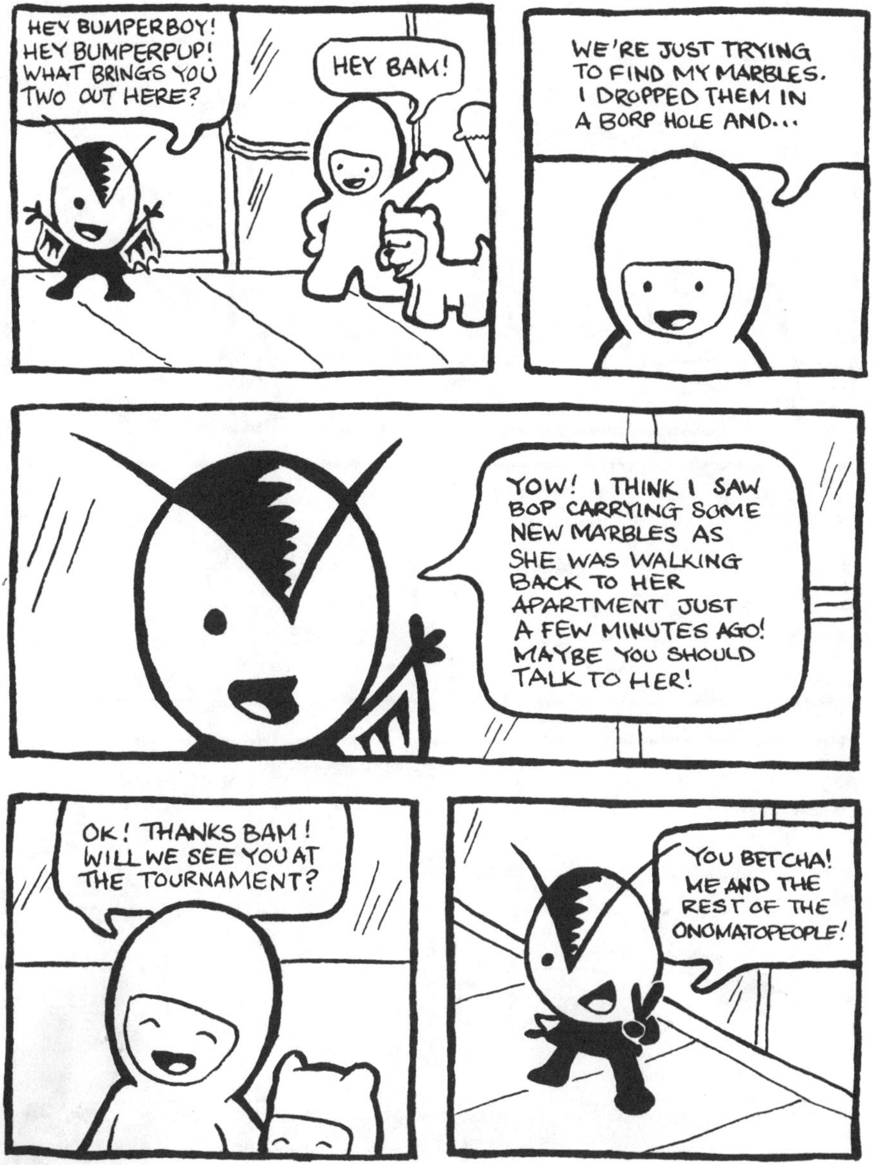
HEY BUMPERBOY! HEY BUMPERPUP! WHAT BRINGS YOU TWO OUT HERE?
HEY BAM!
WE'RE JUST TRYING TO FIND MY MARBLES. I DROPPED THEM IN A BORP HOLE AND...
YOW! I THINK I SAW BOP CARRYING SOME NEW MARBLES AS SHE WAS WALKING BACK TO HER APARTMENT JUST A FEW MINUTES AGO! MAYBE YOU SHOULD TALK TO HER!
OK! THANKS BAM! WILL WE SEE YOU AT THE TOURNAMENT?
YOU BETCHA! ME AND THE REST OF THE ONOMATOPEOPLE!

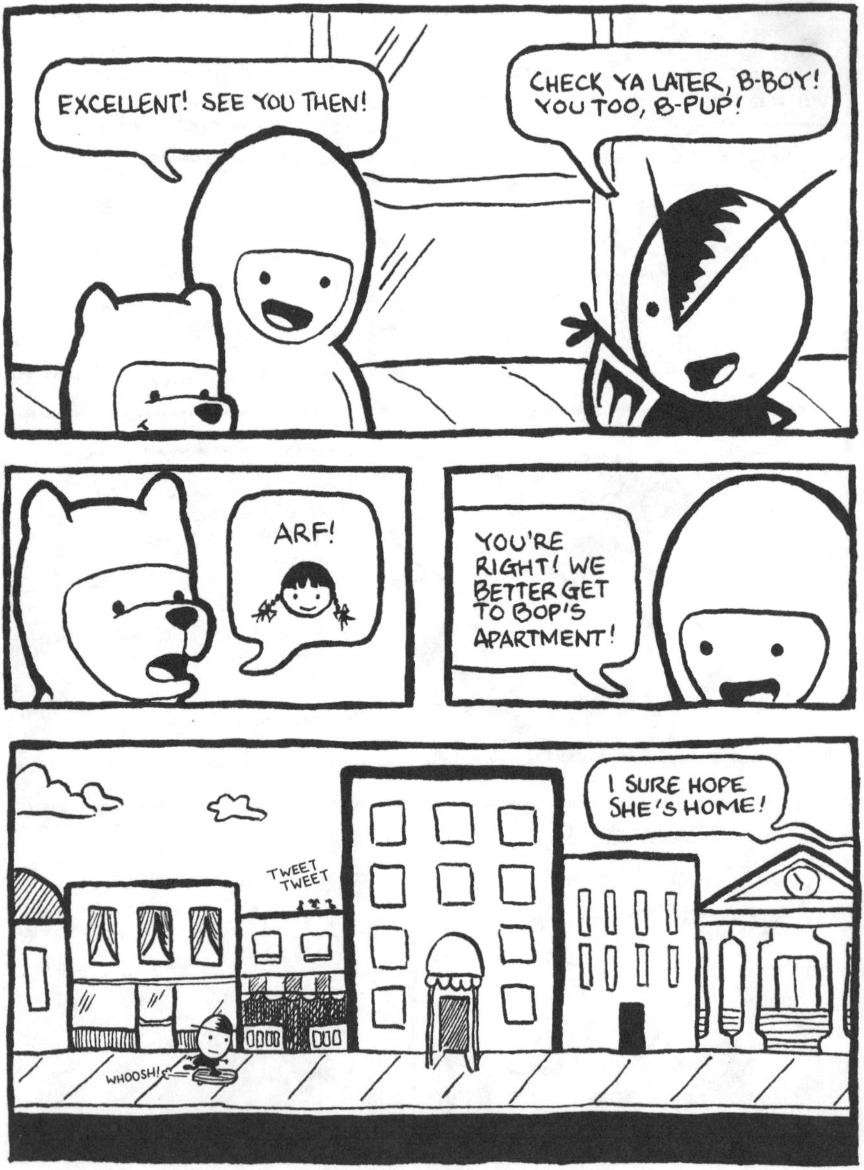
EXCELLENT! SEE YOU THEN!
CHECK YA LATER, B-BOY! YOU TOO, B-PUP!
ARF!
YOU'RE RIGHT! WE BETTER GET TO BOP'S APARTMENT!
I SURE HOPE SHE'S HOME!
TWEET TWEET
WHOOSH!

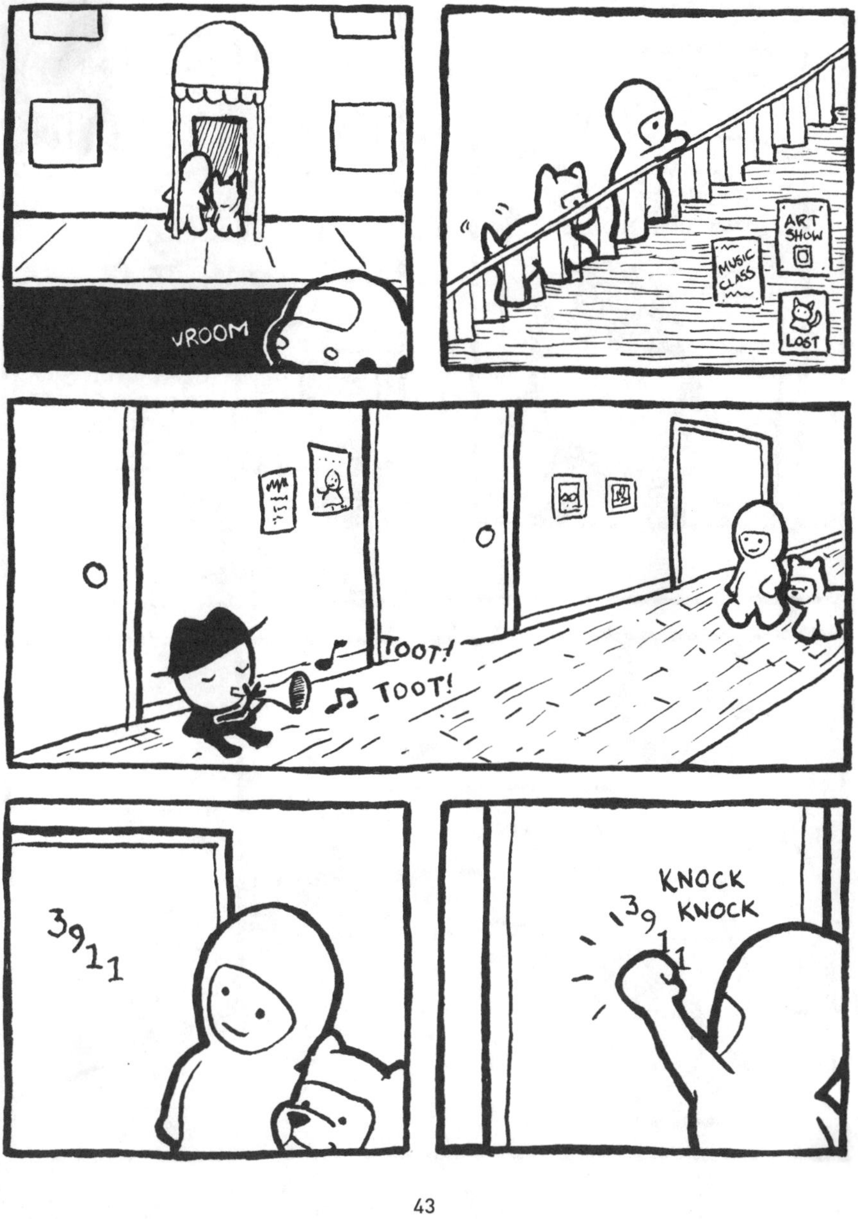
VROOM
ART SHOW
MUSIC CLASS
LOST
TOOT!
TOOT!
3911
KNOCK
KNOCK
3911

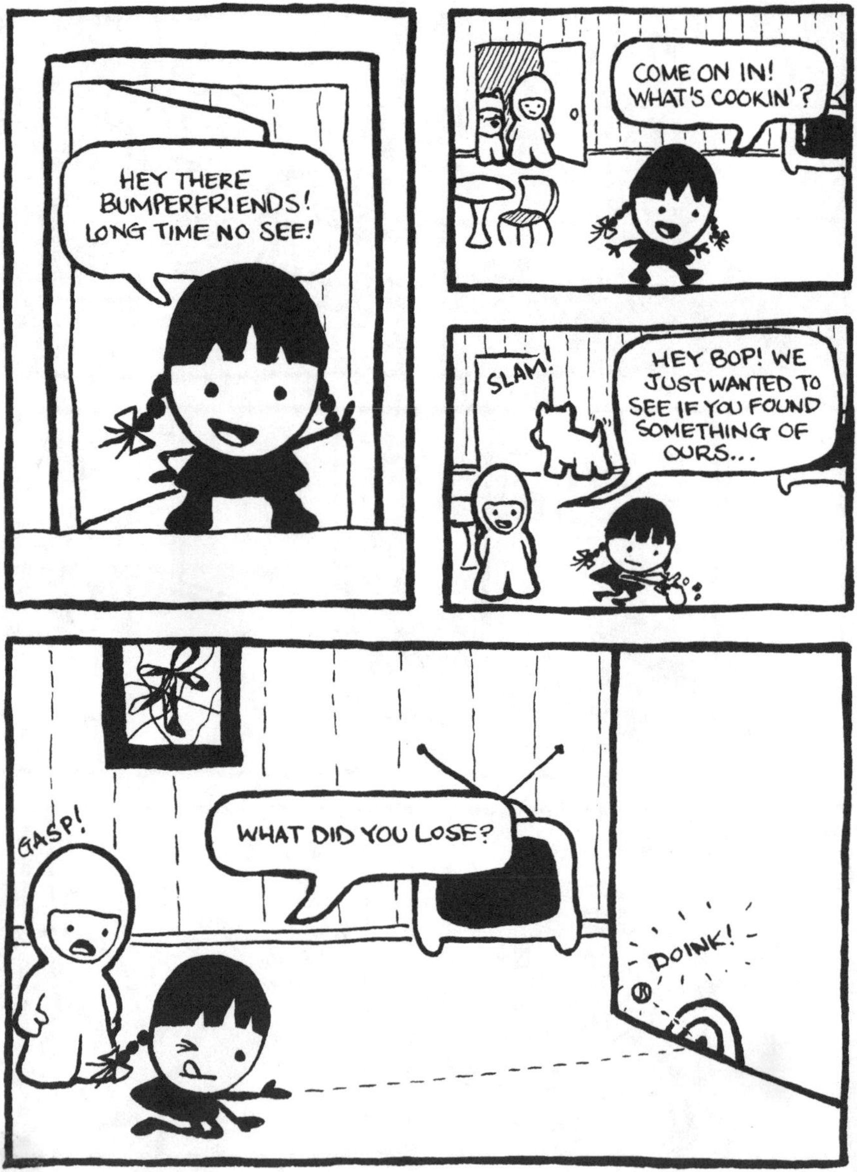
HEY THERE BUMPERFRIENDS! LONG TIME NO SEE!
COME ON IN! WHAT'S COOKIN'?
SLAM!
HEY BOP! WE JUST WANTED TO SEE IF YOU FOUND SOMETHING OF OURS...
GASP!
WHAT DID YOU LOSE?
DOINK!

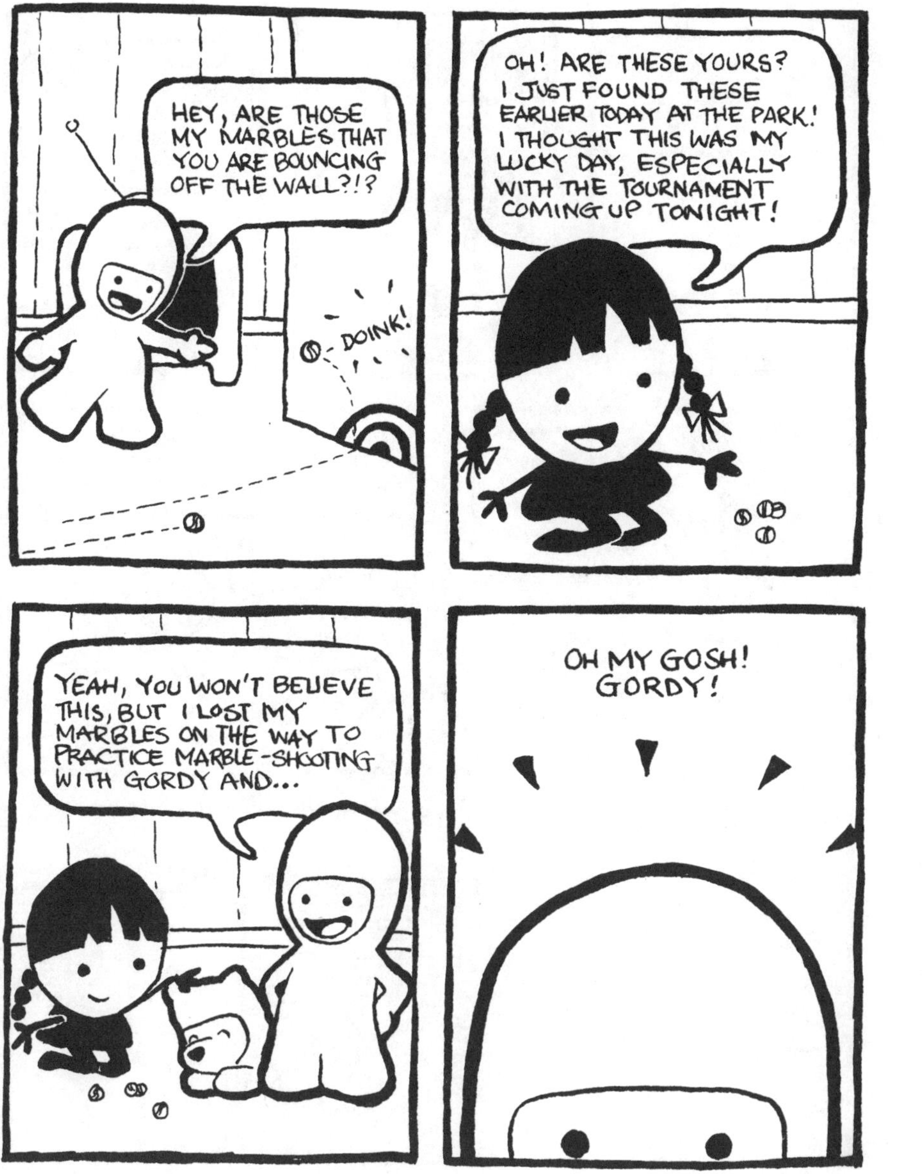
HEY, ARE THOSE MY MARBLES THAT YOU ARE BOUNCING OFF THE WALL?!?
DOINK!
OH! ARE THESE YOURS? I JUST FOUND THESE EARLIER TODAY AT THE PARK! I THOUGHT THIS WAS MY LUCKY DAY, ESPECIALLY WITH THE TOURNAMENT COMING UP TONIGHT!
YEAH, YOU WON'T BELIEVE THIS, BUT I LOST MY MARBLES ON THE WAY TO PRACTICE MARBLE-SHOOTING WITH GORDY AND...
OH MY GOSH! GORDY!

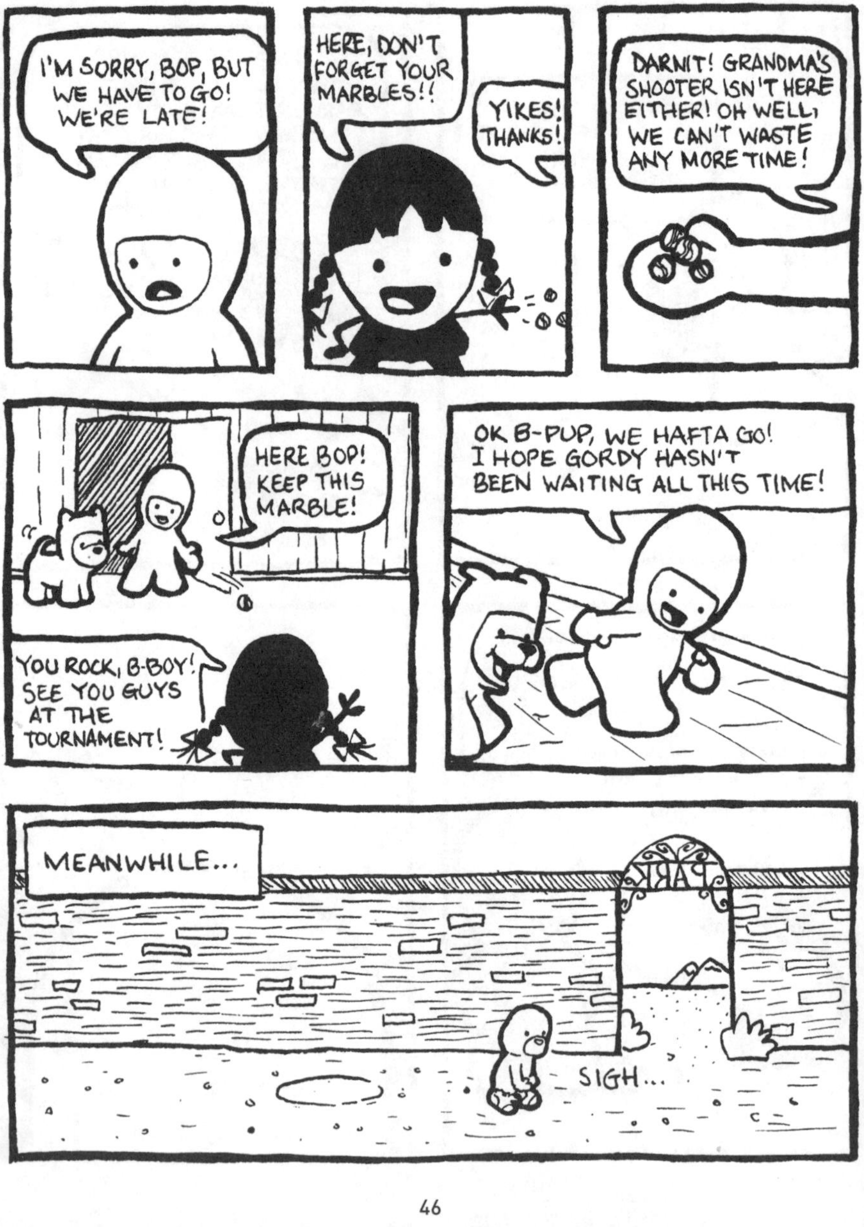

I'M SORRY, BOP, BUT WE HAVE TO GO! WE'RE LATE!
HERE, DON'T FORGET YOUR MARBLES!!
YIKES! THANKS!
DARNIT! GRANDMA'S SHOOTER ISN'T HERE EITHER! OH WELL, WE CAN'T WASTE ANY MORE TIME!
HERE BOP! KEEP THIS MARBLE!
YOU ROCK, B-BOY! SEE YOU GUYS AT THE TOURNAMENT!
OK B-PUP, WE HAFTA GO! I HOPE GORDY HASN'T BEEN WAITING ALL THIS TIME!
MEANWHILE...
PARK
SIGH...

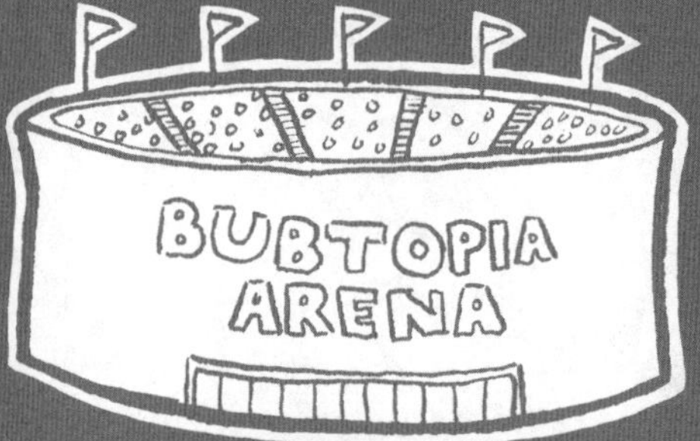
BUBTOPIA
ARENA

PART THREE

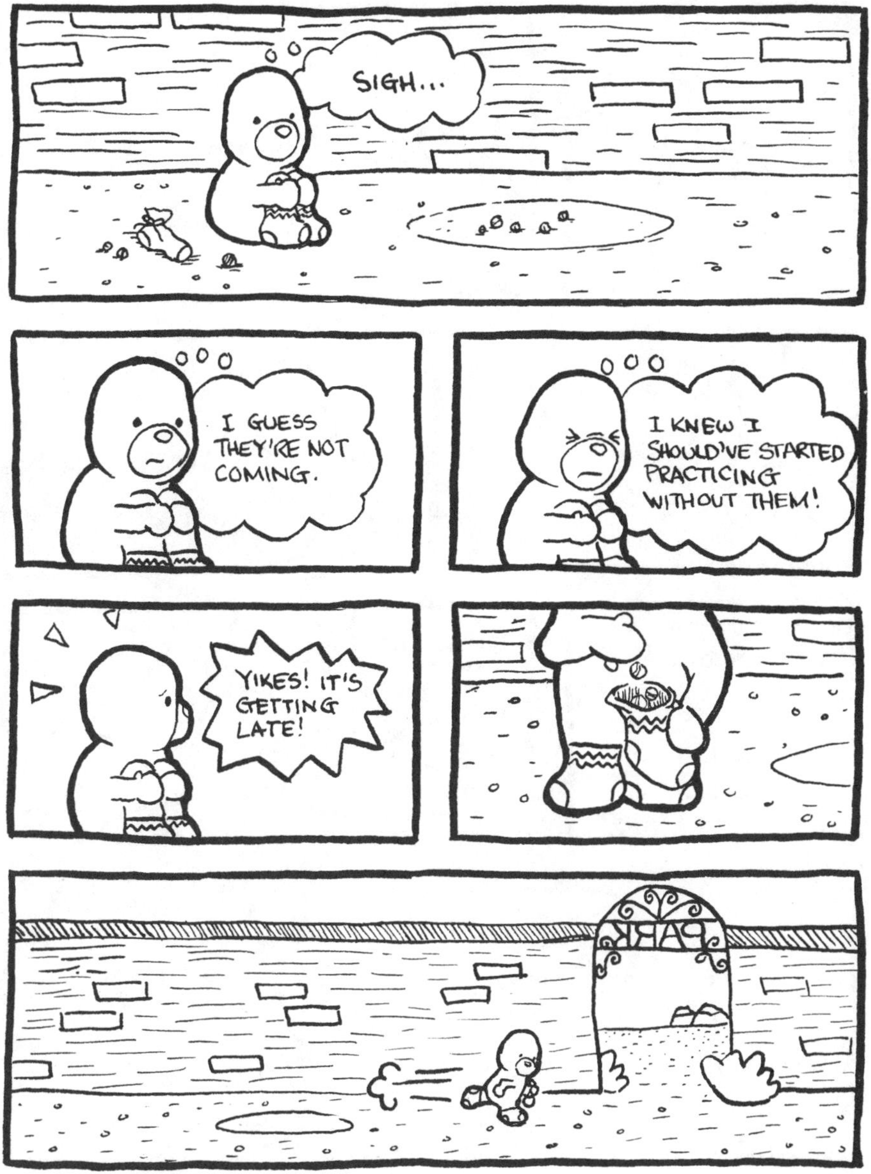
SIGH...
I GUESS THEY'RE NOT COMING.
I KNEW I SHOULD'VE STARTED PRACTICING WITHOUT THEM!
YIKES! IT'S GETTING LATE!
PARK

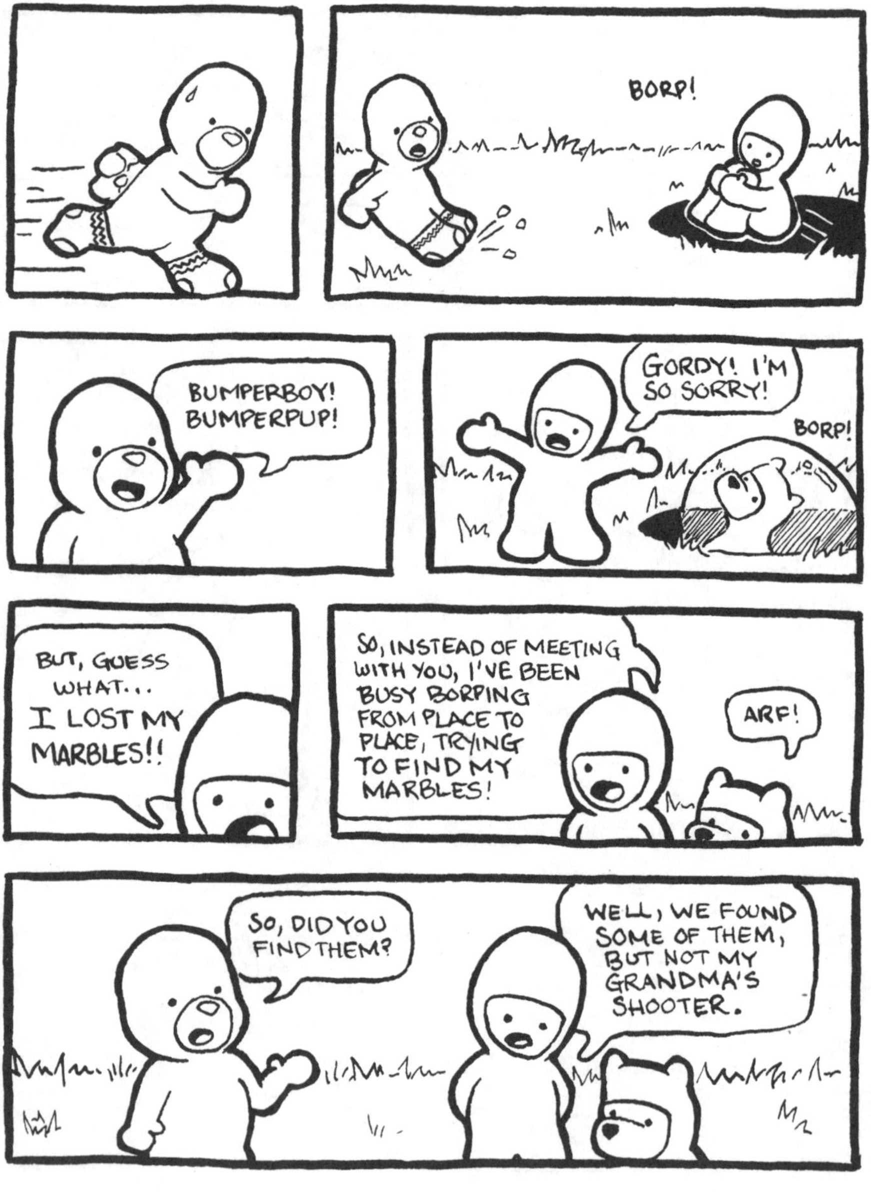
BORP!
BUMPERBOY! BUMPERPUP!
GORDY! I'M SO SORRY!
BORP!
BUT, GUESS WHAT... I LOST MY MARBLES!!
SO, INSTEAD OF MEETING WITH YOU, I'VE BEEN BUSY BORPING FROM PLACE TO PLACE, TRYING TO FIND MY MARBLES!
ARF!
SO, DID YOU FIND THEM?
WELL, WE FOUND SOME OF THEM, BUT NOT MY GRANDMA'S SHOOTER.

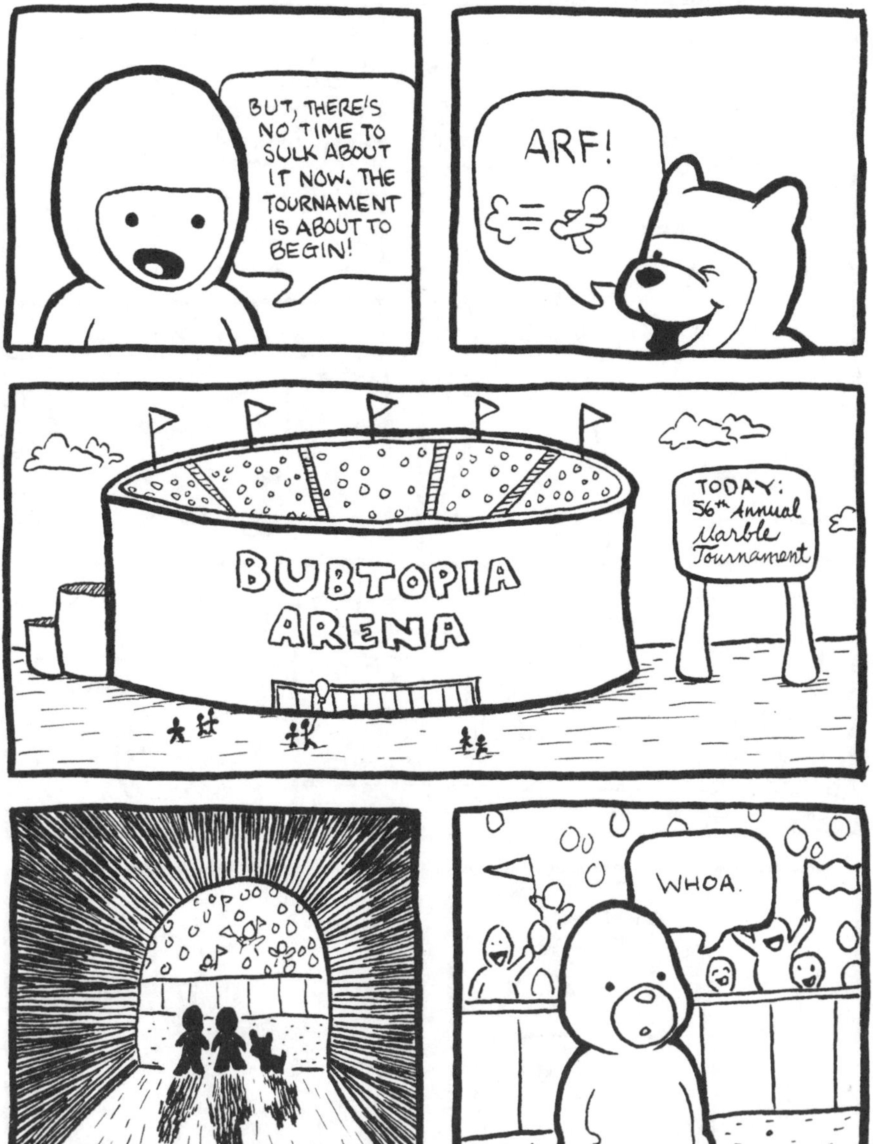
BUT, THERE'S NO TIME TO SULK ABOUT IT NOW. THE TOURNAMENT IS ABOUT TO BEGIN!
ARF!
BUBTOPIA ARENA
TODAY: 56th Annual Marble Tournament
WHOA.

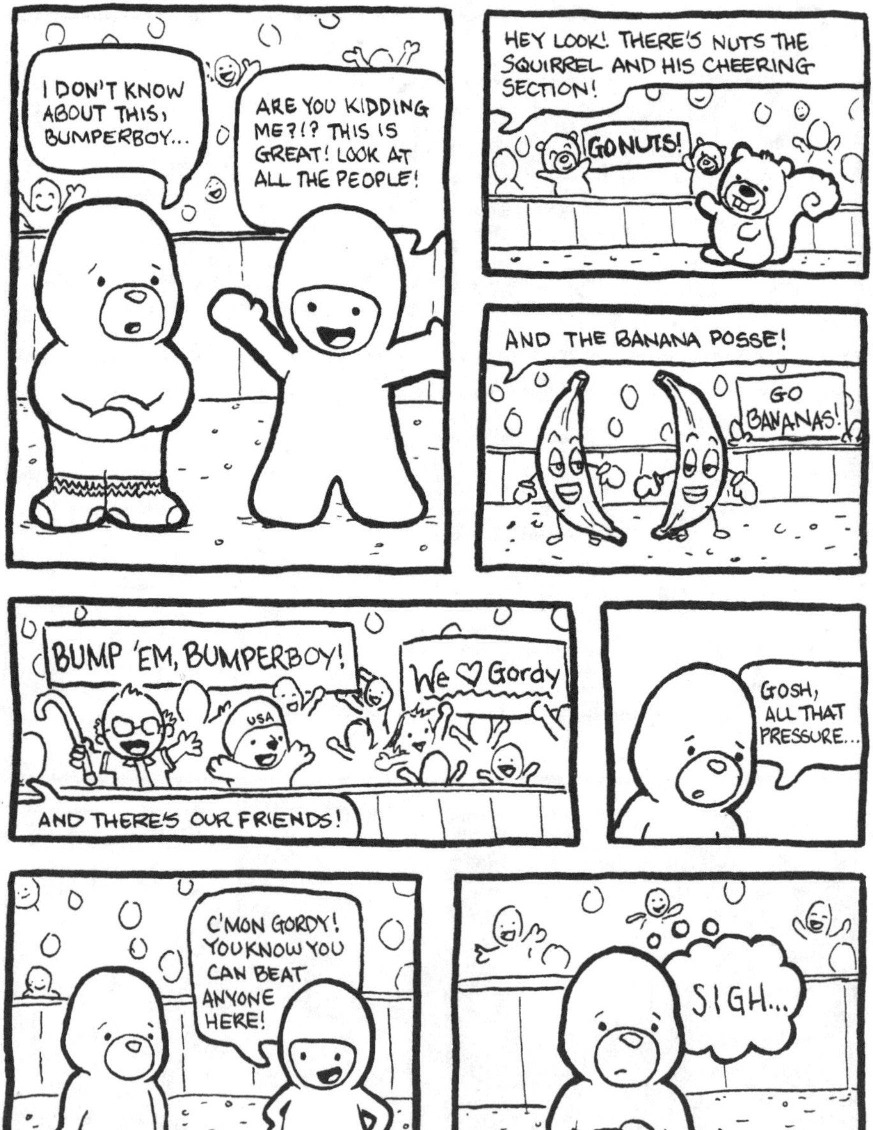
I DON'T KNOW ABOUT THIS, BUMPERBOY...
ARE YOU KIDDING ME?!? THIS IS GREAT! LOOK AT ALL THE PEOPLE!
HEY LOOK! THERE'S NUTS THE SQUIRREL AND HIS CHEERING SECTION!
GO NUTS!
AND THE BANANA POSSE!
GO BANANAS!
BUMP 'EM, BUMPERBOY!
USA
We ♡ Gordy
AND THERE'S OUR FRIENDS!
GOSH, ALL THAT PRESSURE...
C'MON GORDY! YOU KNOW YOU CAN BEAT ANYONE HERE!
SIGH...

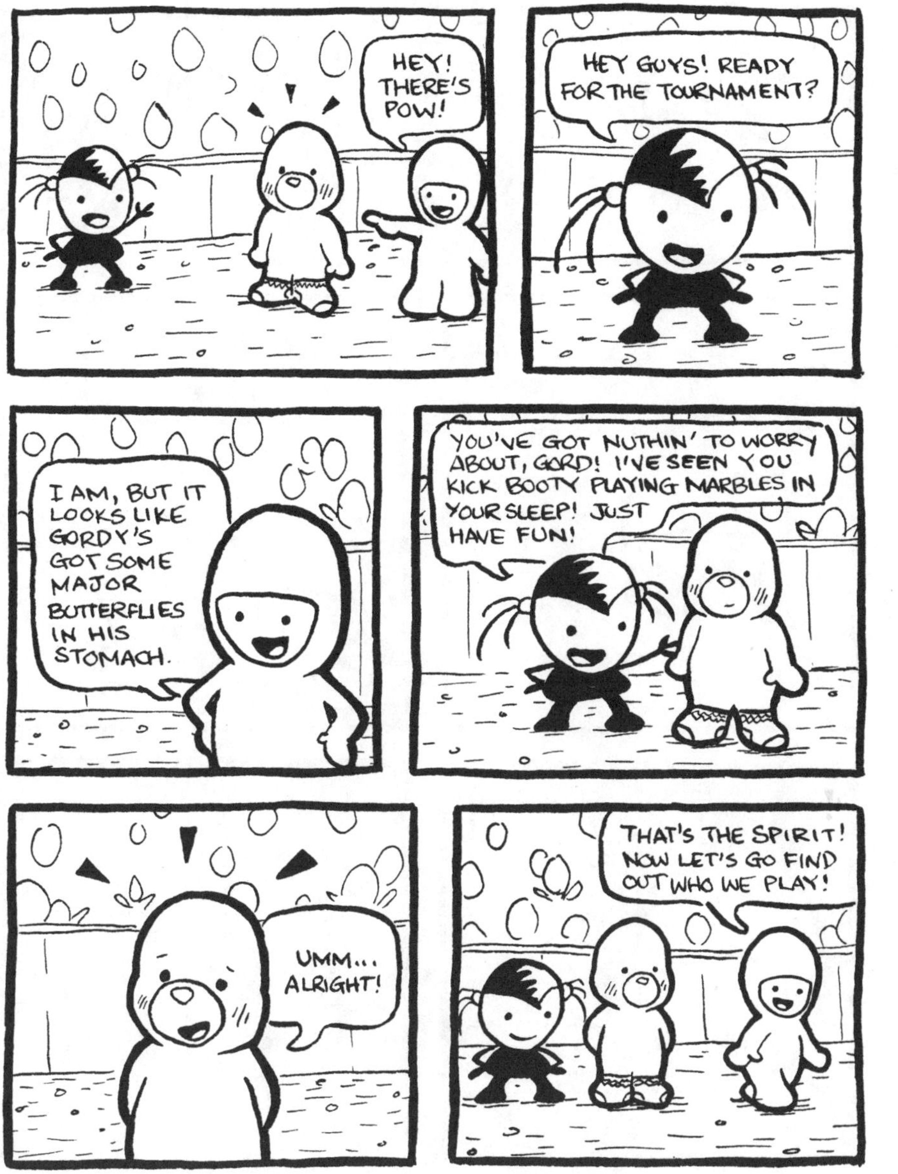
HEY! THERE'S POW!
HEY GUYS! READY FOR THE TOURNAMENT?
I AM, BUT IT LOOKS LIKE GORDY'S GOT SOME MAJOR BUTTERFLIES IN HIS STOMACH.
YOU'VE GOT NUTHIN' TO WORRY ABOUT, GORD! I'VE SEEN YOU KICK BOOTY PLAYING MARBLES IN YOUR SLEEP! JUST HAVE FUN!
UMM... ALRIGHT!
THAT'S THE SPIRIT! NOW LET'S GO FIND OUT WHO WE PLAY!

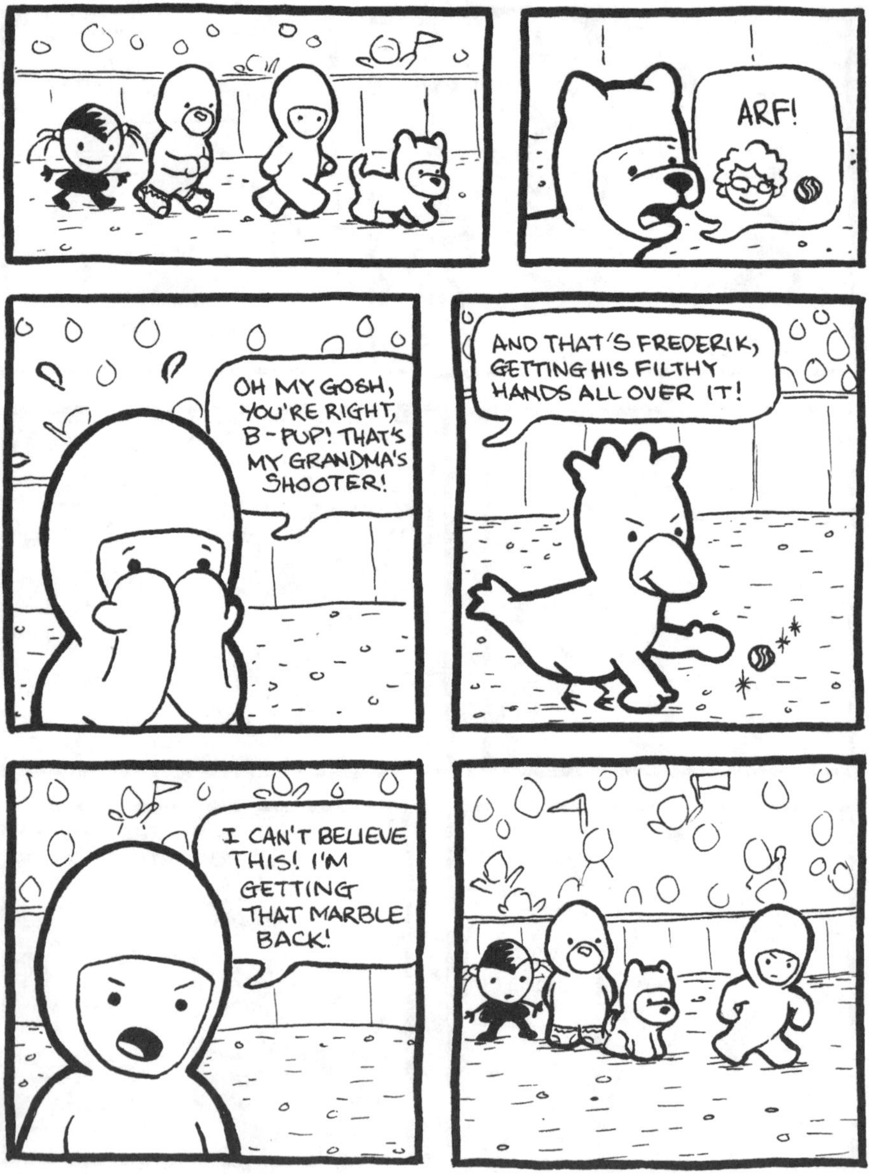
ARF!
OH MY GOSH, YOU'RE RIGHT, B-PUP! THAT'S MY GRANDMA'S SHOOTER!
AND THAT'S FREDERIK, GETTING HIS FILTHY HANDS ALL OVER IT!
I CAN'T BELIEVE THIS! I'M GETTING THAT MARBLE BACK!

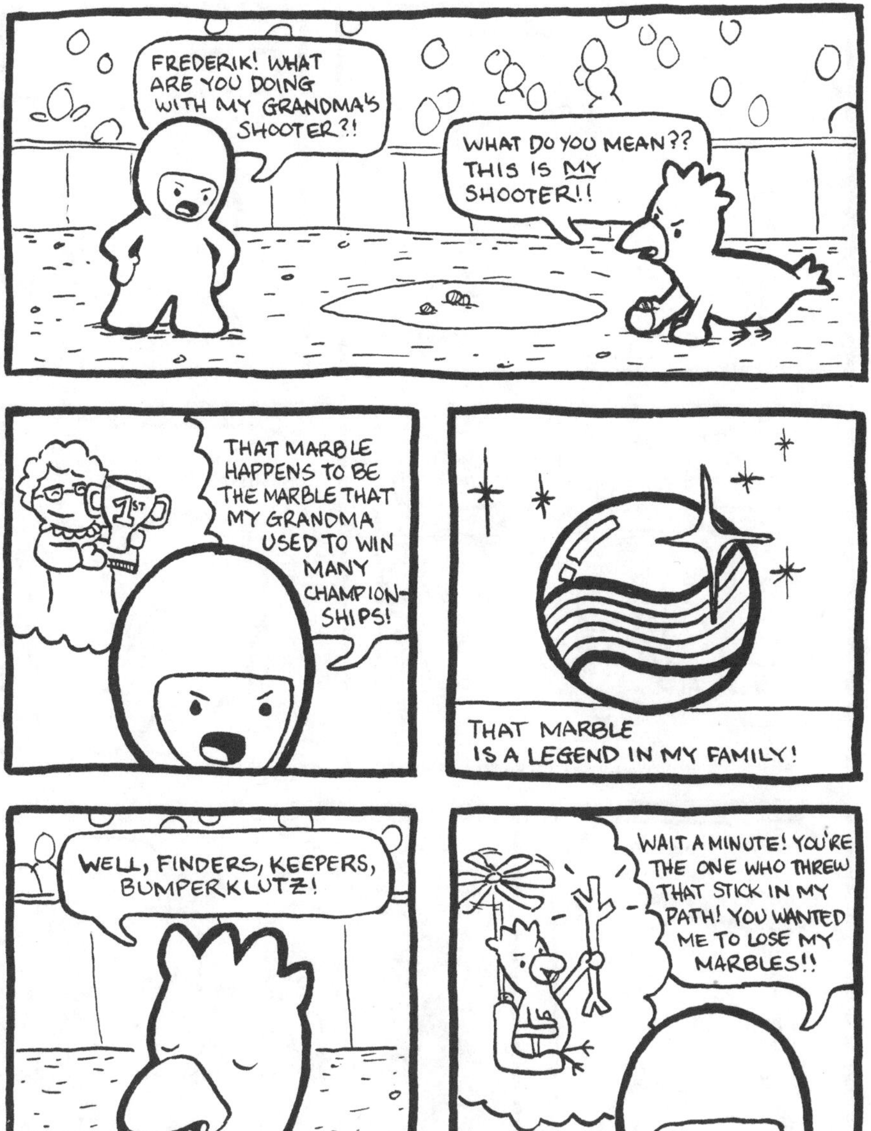
FREDERIK! WHAT ARE YOU DOING WITH MY GRANDMA'S SHOOTER?!
WHAT DO YOU MEAN?? THIS IS MY SHOOTER!!
THAT MARBLE HAPPENS TO BE THE MARBLE THAT MY GRANDMA USED TO WIN MANY CHAMPIONSHIPS!
1ST
THAT MARBLE IS A LEGEND IN MY FAMILY!
WELL, FINDERS, KEEPERS, BUMPERKLUTZ!
WAIT A MINUTE! YOU'RE THE ONE WHO THREW THAT STICK IN MY PATH! YOU WANTED ME TO LOSE MY MARBLES!!

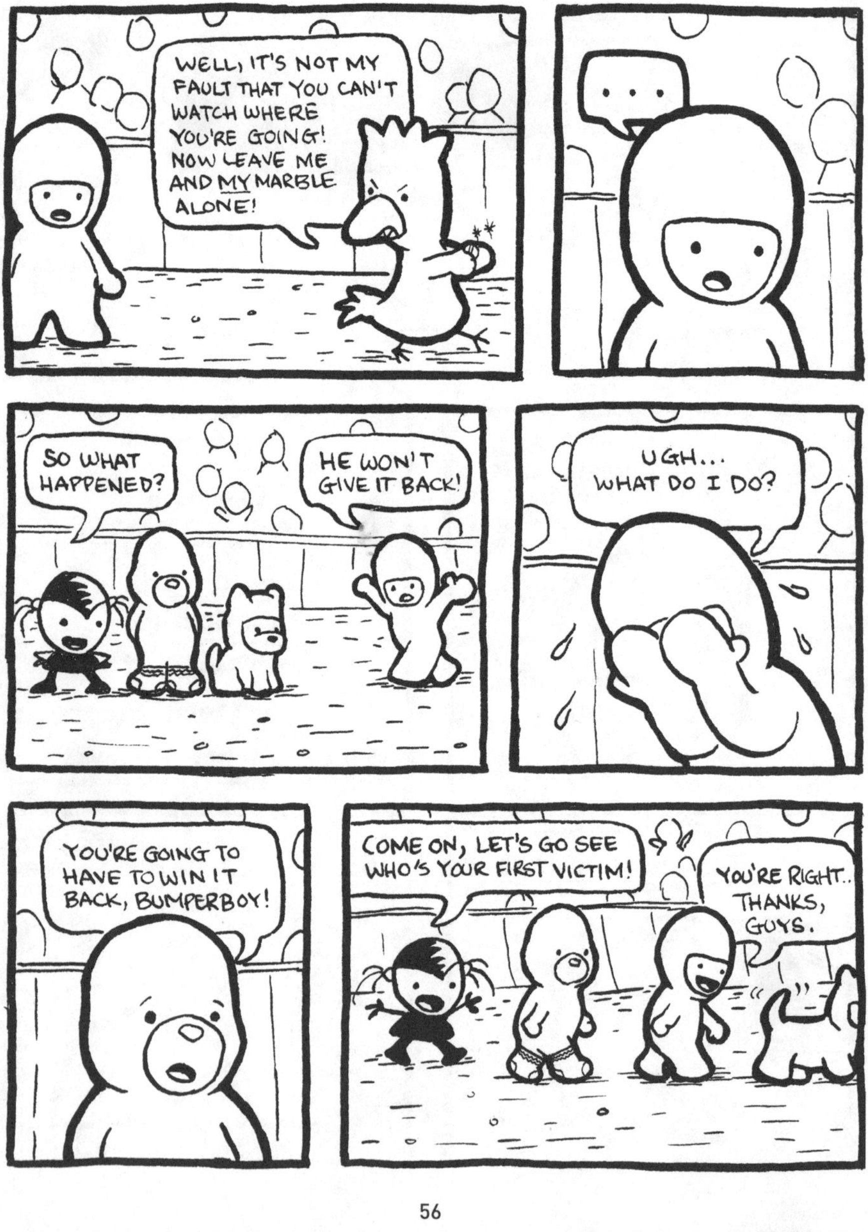
WELL, IT'S NOT MY FAULT THAT YOU CAN'T WATCH WHERE YOU'RE GOING! NOW LEAVE ME AND MY MARBLE ALONE!
...
SO WHAT HAPPENED?
HE WON'T GIVE IT BACK!
UGH... WHAT DO I DO?
YOU'RE GOING TO HAVE TO WIN IT BACK, BUMPERBOY!
COME ON, LET'S GO SEE WHO'S YOUR FIRST VICTIM!
YOU'RE RIGHT.. THANKS, GUYS.

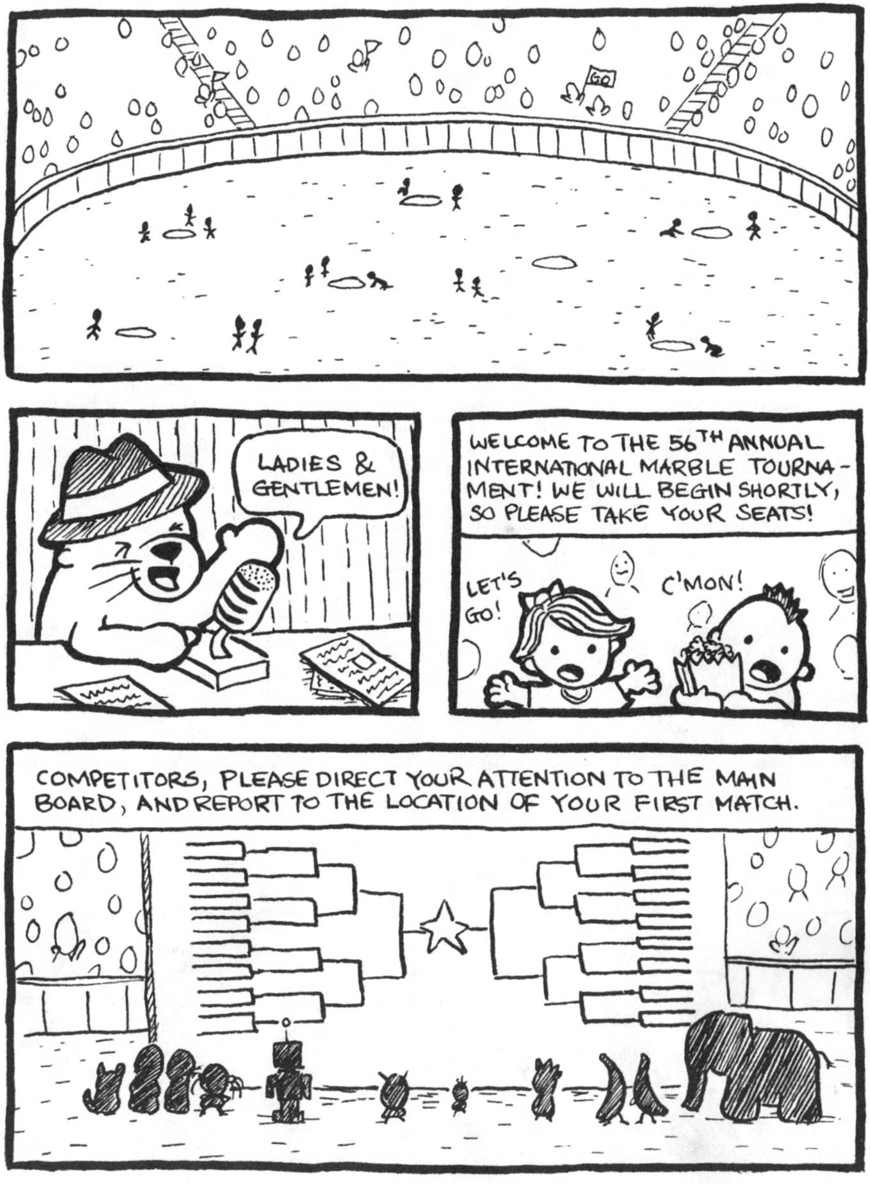
GO
LADIES & GENTLEMEN!
WELCOME TO THE 56TH ANNUAL INTERNATIONAL MARBLE TOURNAMENT! WE WILL BEGIN SHORTLY, SO PLEASE TAKE YOUR SEATS!
LET'S GO!
C'MON!
COMPETITORS, PLEASE DIRECT YOUR ATTENTION TO THE MAIN BOARD, AND REPORT TO THE LOCATION OF YOUR FIRST MATCH.

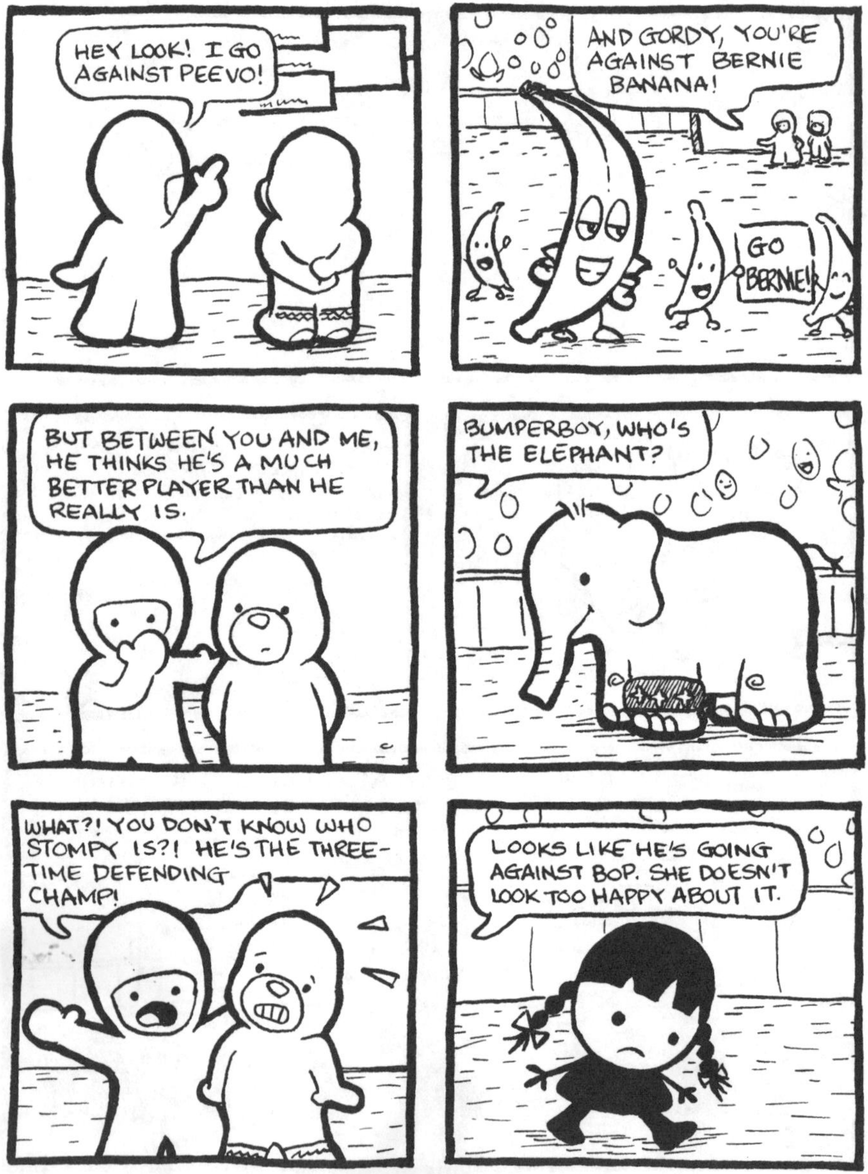
HEY LOOK! I GO AGAINST PEEVO!
AND GORDY, YOU'RE AGAINST BERNIE BANANA!
GO BERNIE!
BUT BETWEEN YOU AND ME, HE THINKS HE'S A MUCH BETTER PLAYER THAN HE REALLY IS.
BUMPERBOY, WHO'S THE ELEPHANT?
WHAT?! YOU DON'T KNOW WHO STOMPY IS?! HE'S THE THREE-TIME DEFENDING CHAMP!
LOOKS LIKE HE'S GOING AGAINST BOP. SHE DOESN'T LOOK TOO HAPPY ABOUT IT.

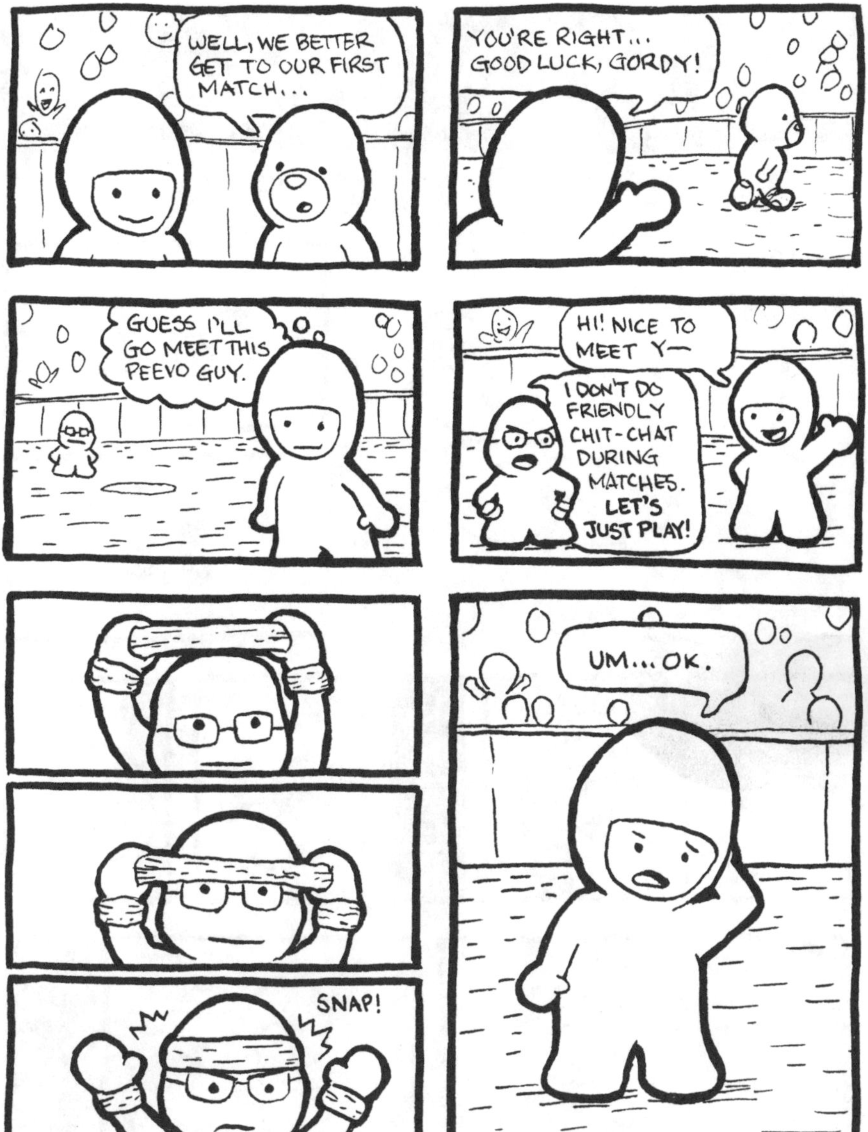
WELL, WE BETTER GET TO OUR FIRST MATCH...
YOU'RE RIGHT... GOOD LUCK, GORDY!
GUESS I'LL GO MEET THIS PEEVO GUY.
HI! NICE TO MEET Y—
I DON'T DO FRIENDLY CHIT-CHAT DURING MATCHES. LET'S JUST PLAY!
SNAP!
UM... OK.

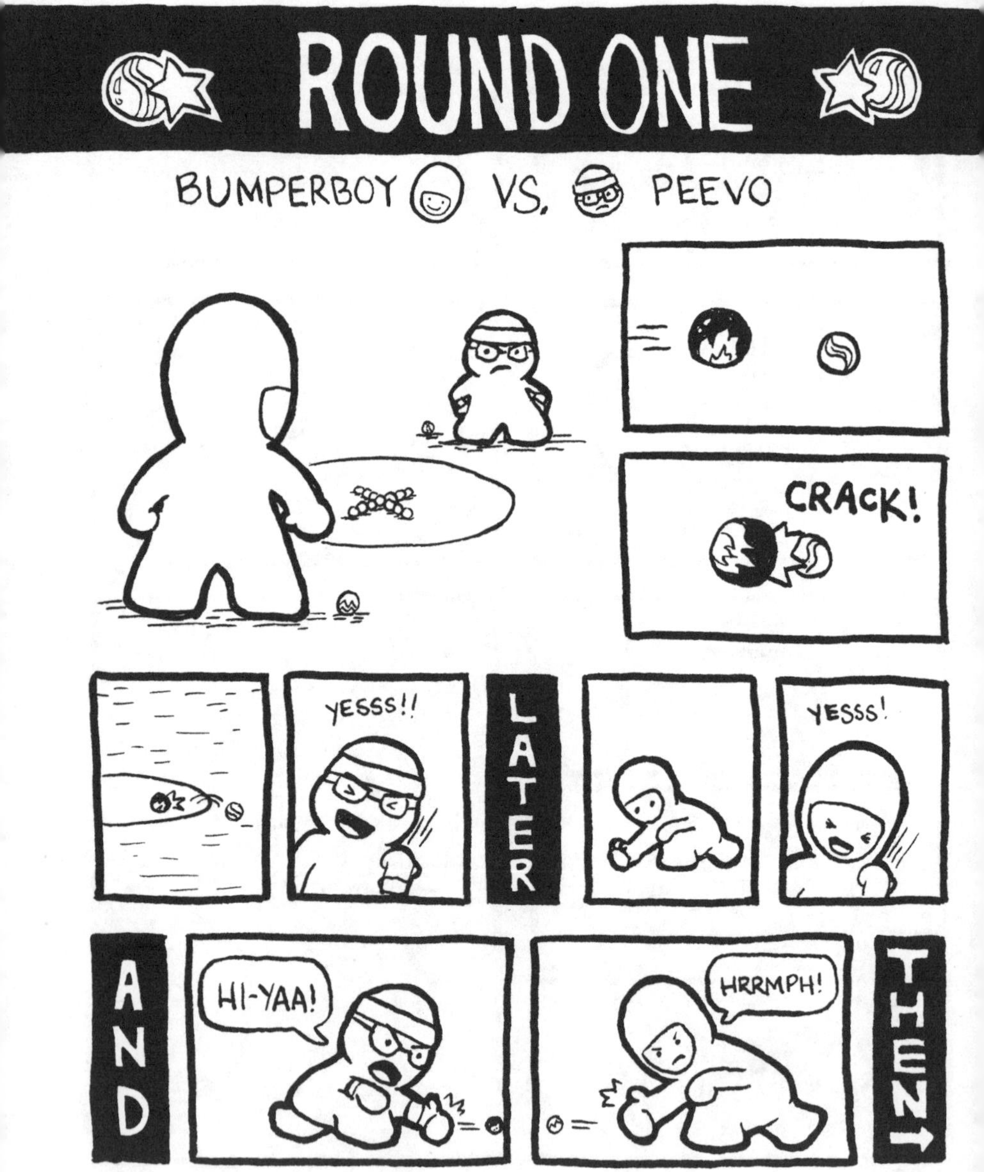
ROUND ONE
BUMPERBOY VS. PEEVO
CRACK!
YESSS!!
LATER
YESSS!
AND
HI-YAA!
HRRMPH!
THEN

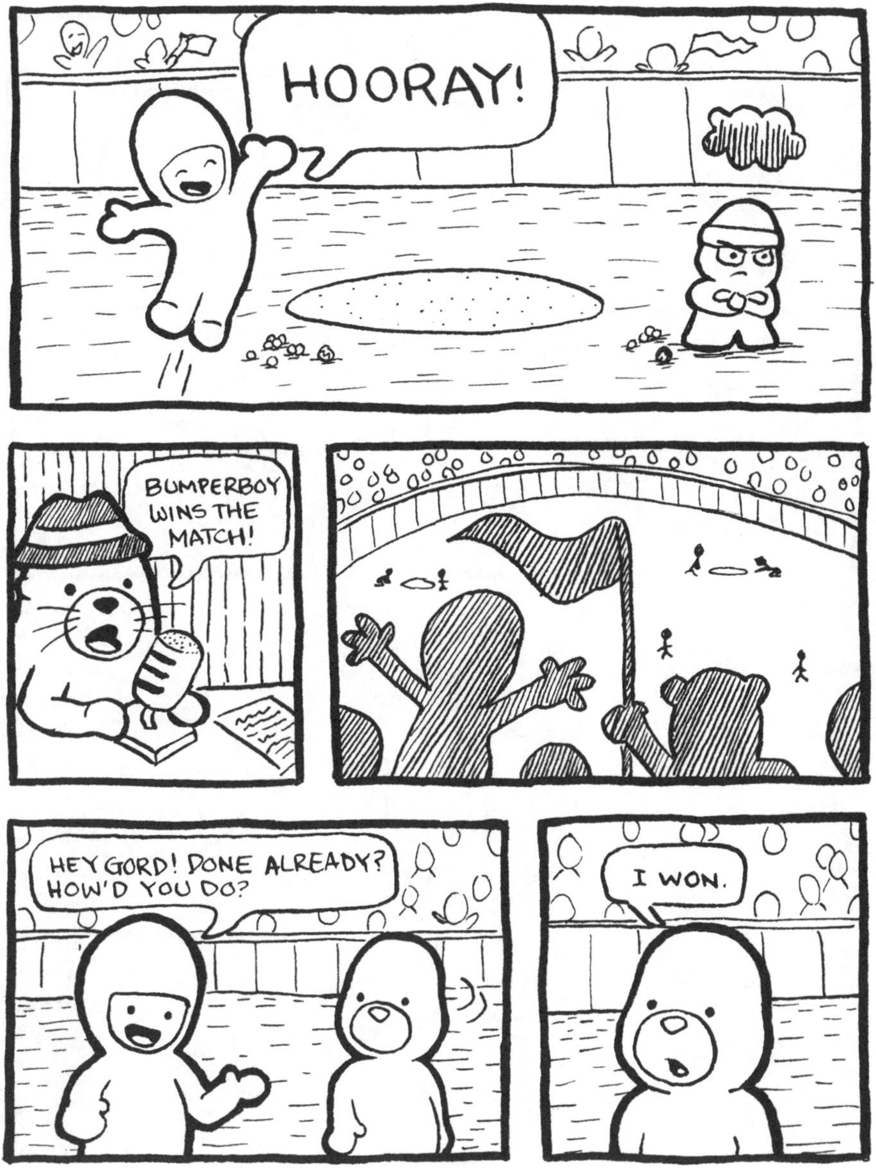
HOORAY!
BUMPERBOY WINS THE MATCH!
HEY GORD! DONE ALREADY? HOW'D YOU DO?
I WON.

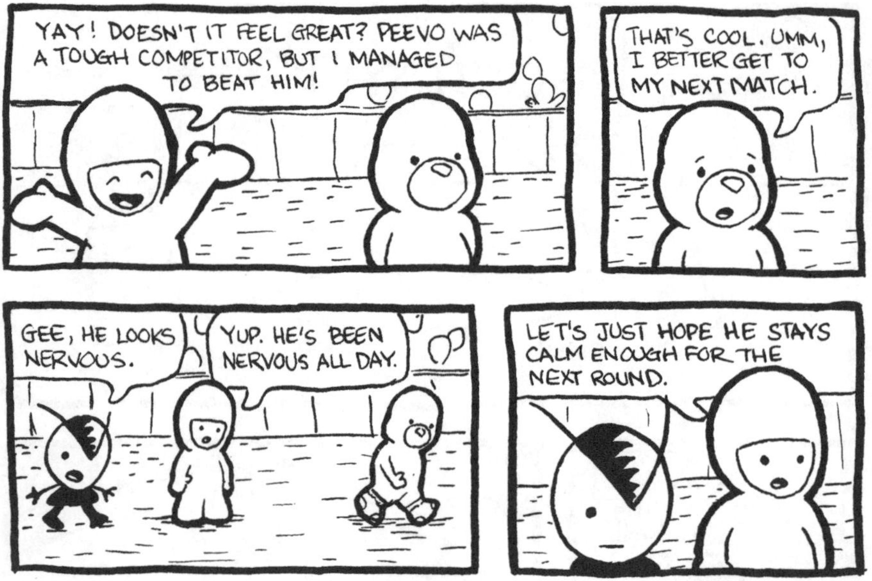
YAY! DOESN'T IT FEEL GREAT? PEEVO WAS A TOUGH COMPETITOR, BUT I MANAGED TO BEAT HIM!
THAT'S COOL. UMM, I BETTER GET TO MY NEXT MATCH.
GEE, HE LOOKS NERVOUS.
YUP. HE'S BEEN NERVOUS ALL DAY.
LET'S JUST HOPE HE STAYS CALM ENOUGH FOR THE NEXT ROUND.

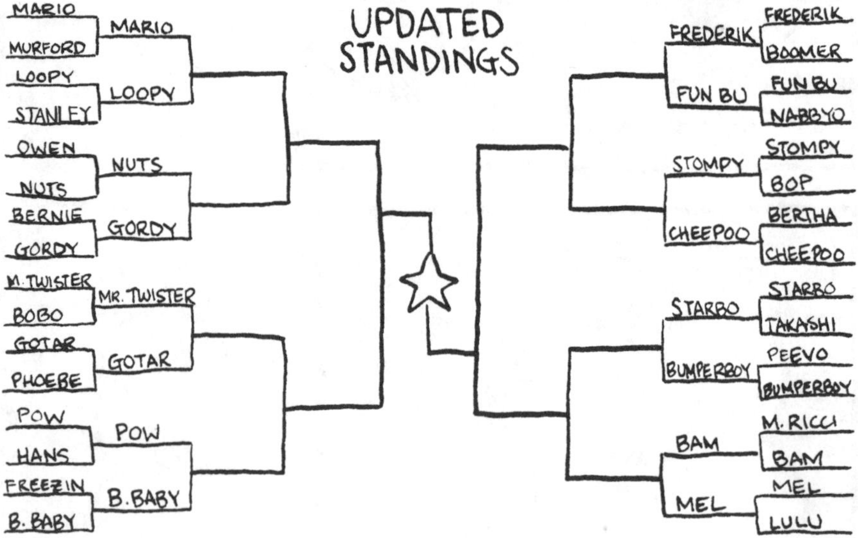
UPDATED STANDINGS
MARIO
MURFORD
MARIO
LOOPY
STANLEY
LOOPY
OWEN
NUTS
NUTS
BERNIE
GORDY
GORDY
M.TWISTER
BOBO
MR. TWISTER
GOTAR
PHOEBE
GOTAR
POW
HANS
POW
FREEZIN
B. BABY
B. BABY
FREDERIK
BOOMER
FREDERIK
FUN BU
NABBYO
FUN BU
STOMPY
BOP
STOMPY
BERTHA
CHEEPOO
CHEEPOO
STARBO
TAKASHI
STARBO
PEEVO
BUMPERBOY
BUMPERBOY
M. RICCI
BAM
BAM
MEL
LULU
MEL

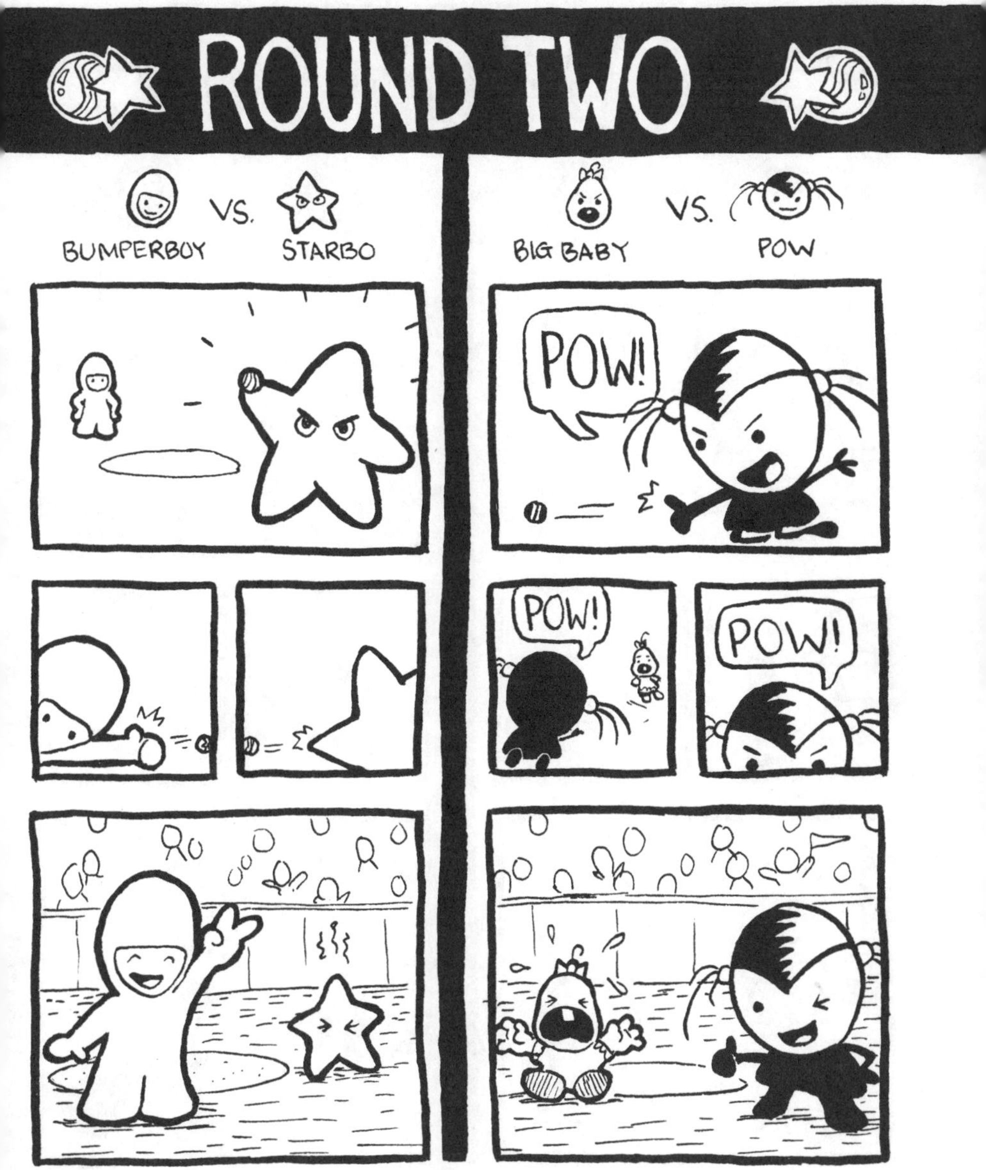
ROUND TWO
BUMPERBOY VS. STARBO
BIG BABY VS. POW
POW!
POW!
POW!

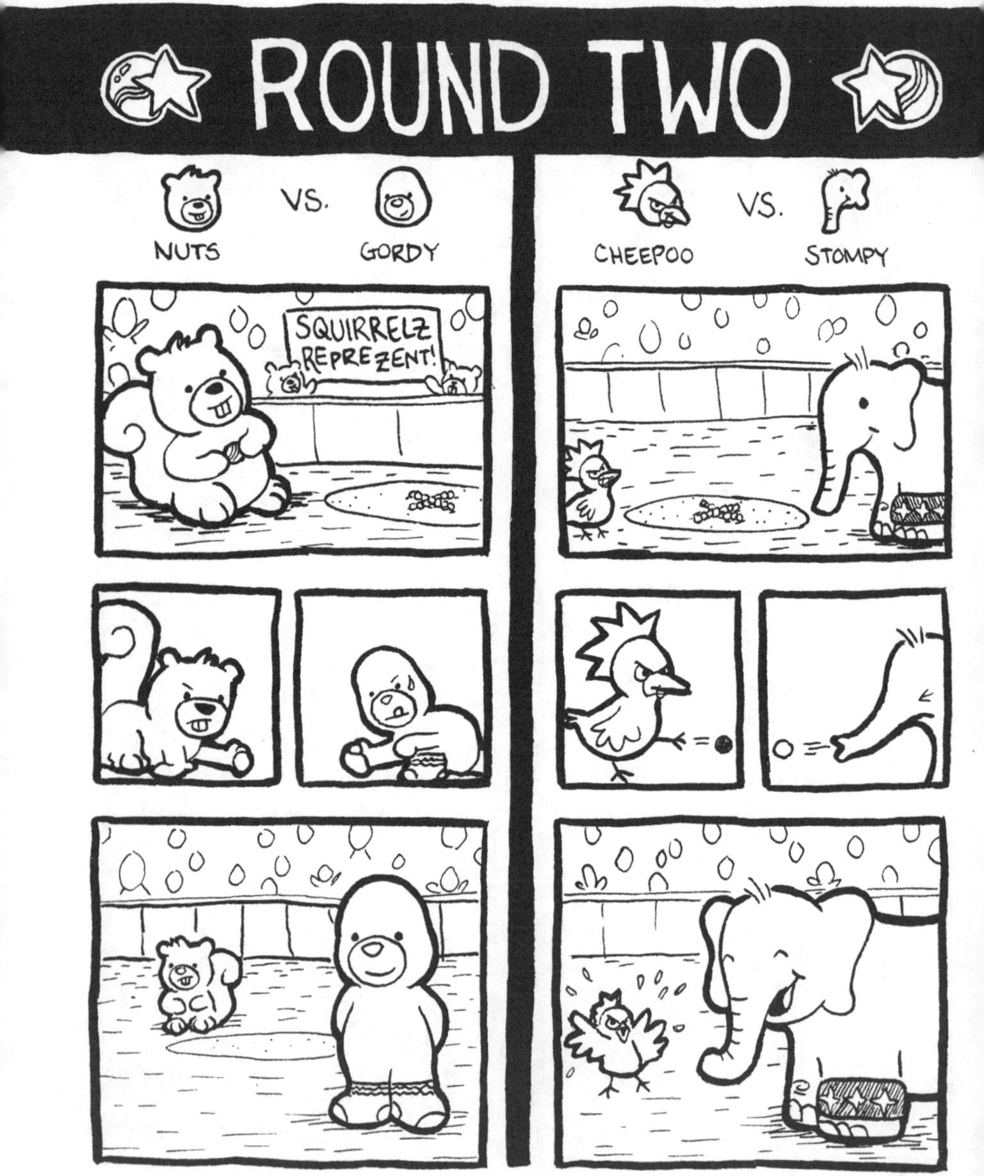
ROUND TWO
NUTS
VS.
GORDY
CHEEPOO
VS.
STOMPY
SQUIRRELZ REPREZENT!

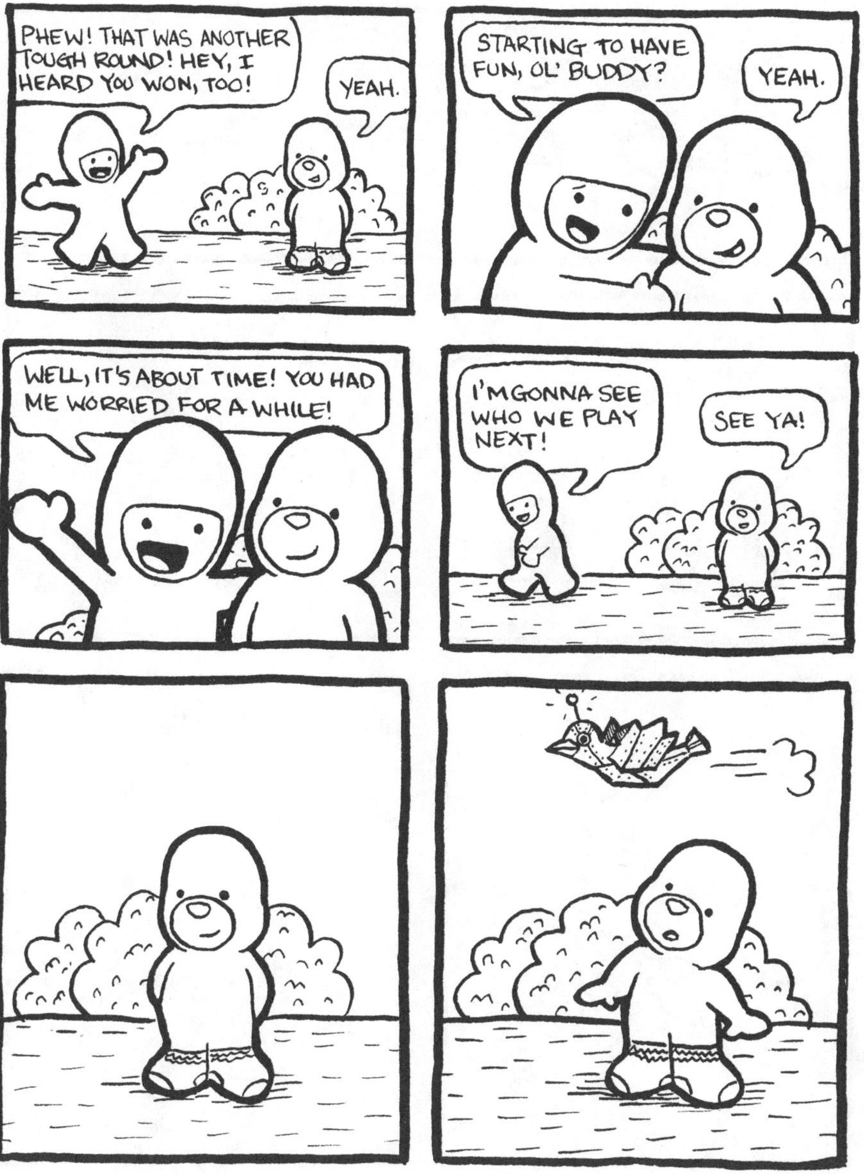
PHEW! THAT WAS ANOTHER TOUGH ROUND! HEY, I HEARD YOU WON, TOO!
YEAH.
STARTING TO HAVE FUN, OL' BUDDY?
YEAH.
WELL, IT'S ABOUT TIME! YOU HAD ME WORRIED FOR A WHILE!
I'M GONNA SEE WHO WE PLAY NEXT!
SEE YA!

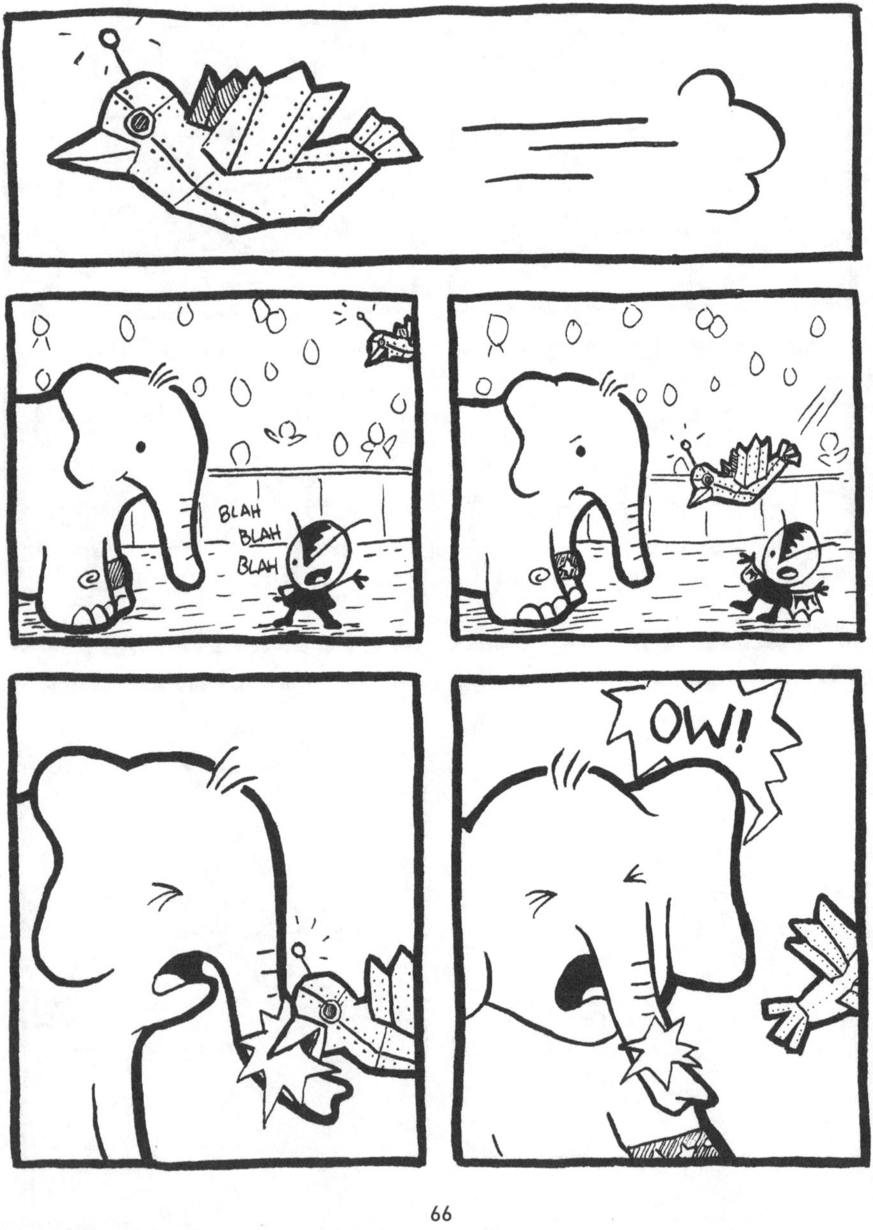
BLAH
BLAH
BLAH
OW!

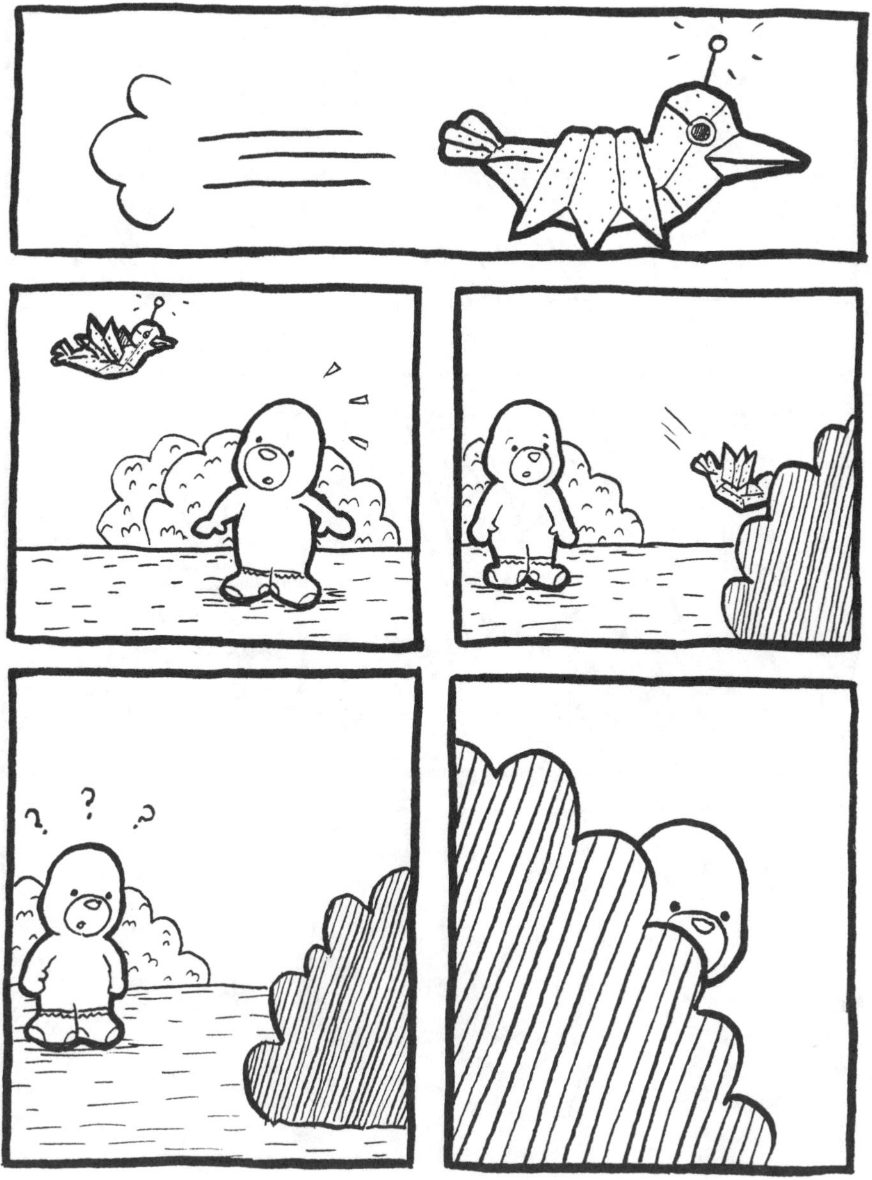
? ? ?

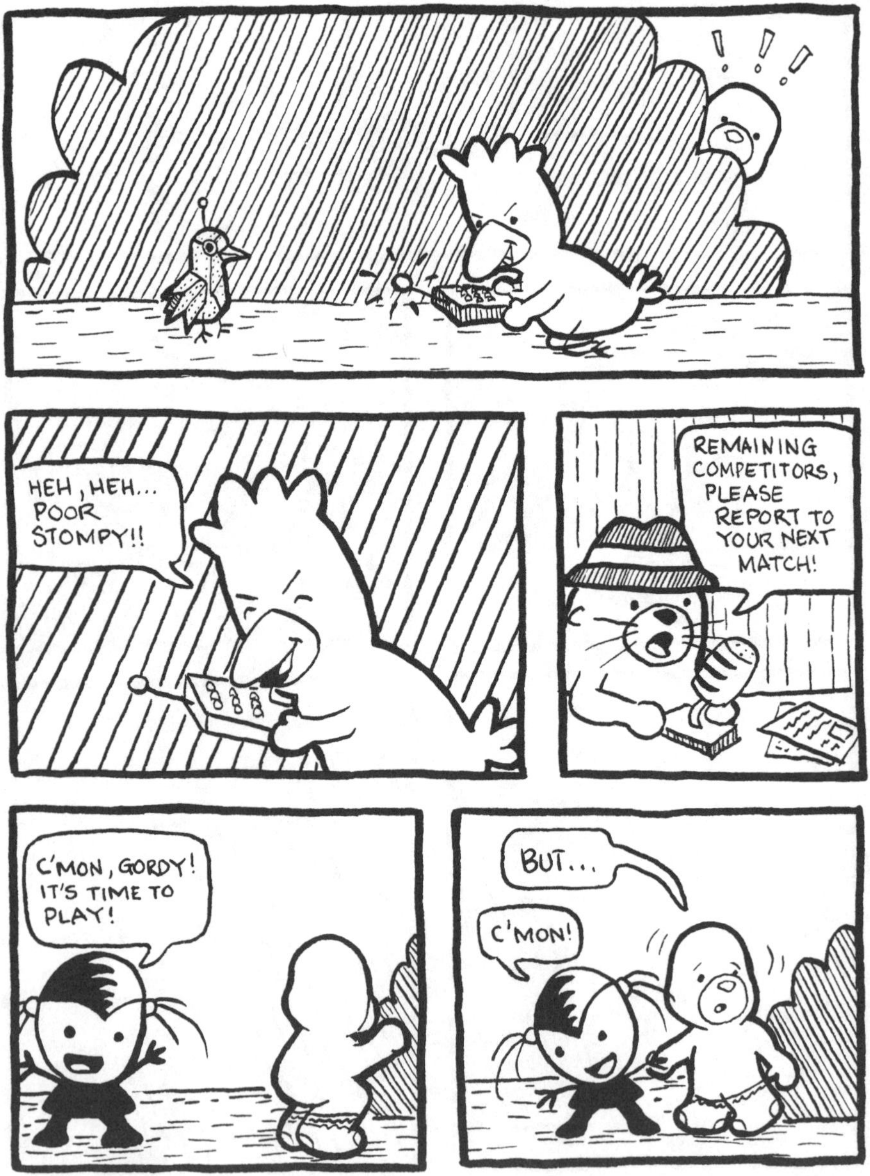
!!!
HEH, HEH... POOR STOMPY!!
REMAINING COMPETITORS, PLEASE REPORT TO YOUR NEXT MATCH!
C'MON, GORDY! IT'S TIME TO PLAY!
BUT...
C'MON!

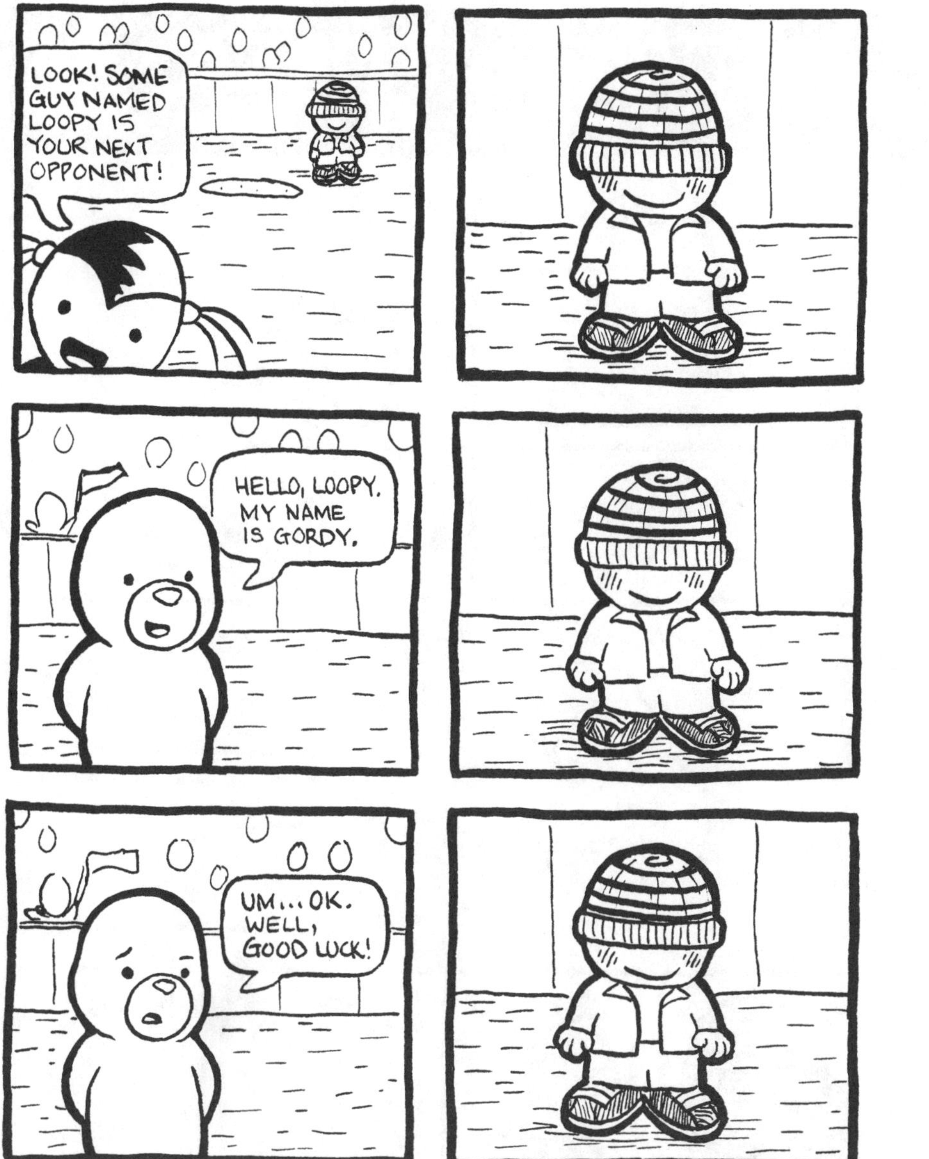
LOOK! SOME GUY NAMED LOOPY IS YOUR NEXT OPPONENT!
HELLO, LOOPY. MY NAME IS GORDY.
UM... OK. WELL, GOOD LUCK!

ROUND THREE

GORDY VS. LOOPY

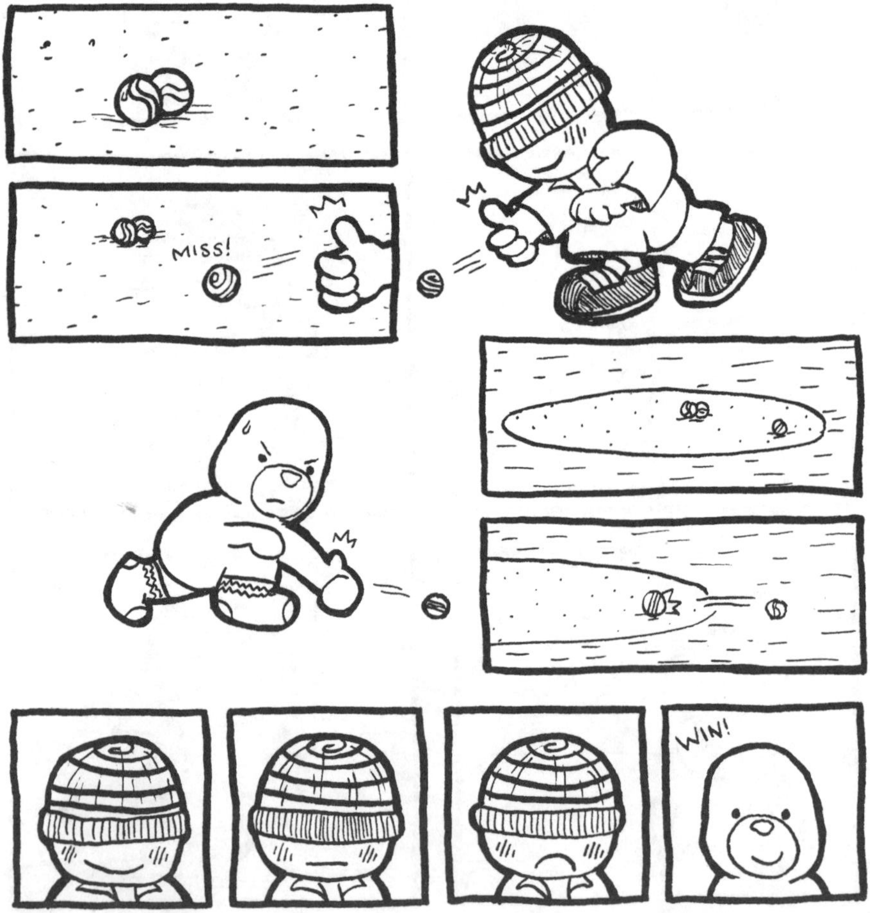
MISS!
WIN!

ROUND THREE

GOTAR™ THE ROBOT VS. POW

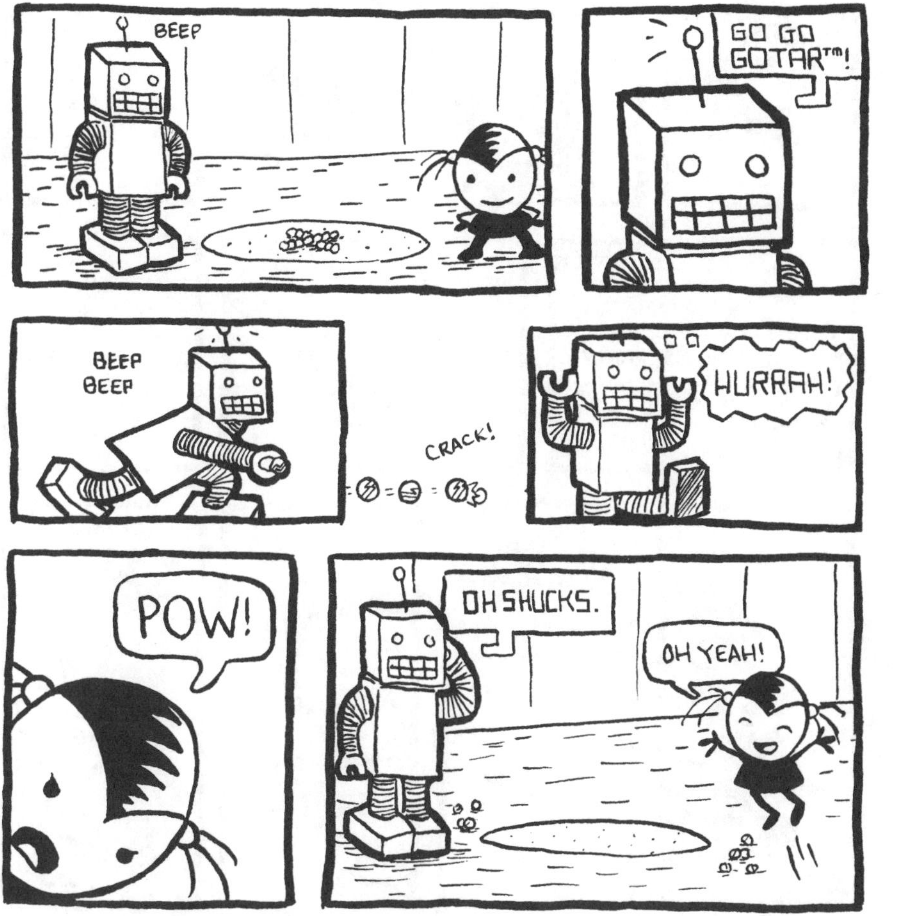
BEEP
GO GO GOTAR™!
BEEP BEEP
CRACK!
HURRAH!
POW!
OH SHUCKS.
OH YEAH!

ROUND THREE

BAM VS. BUMPERBOY

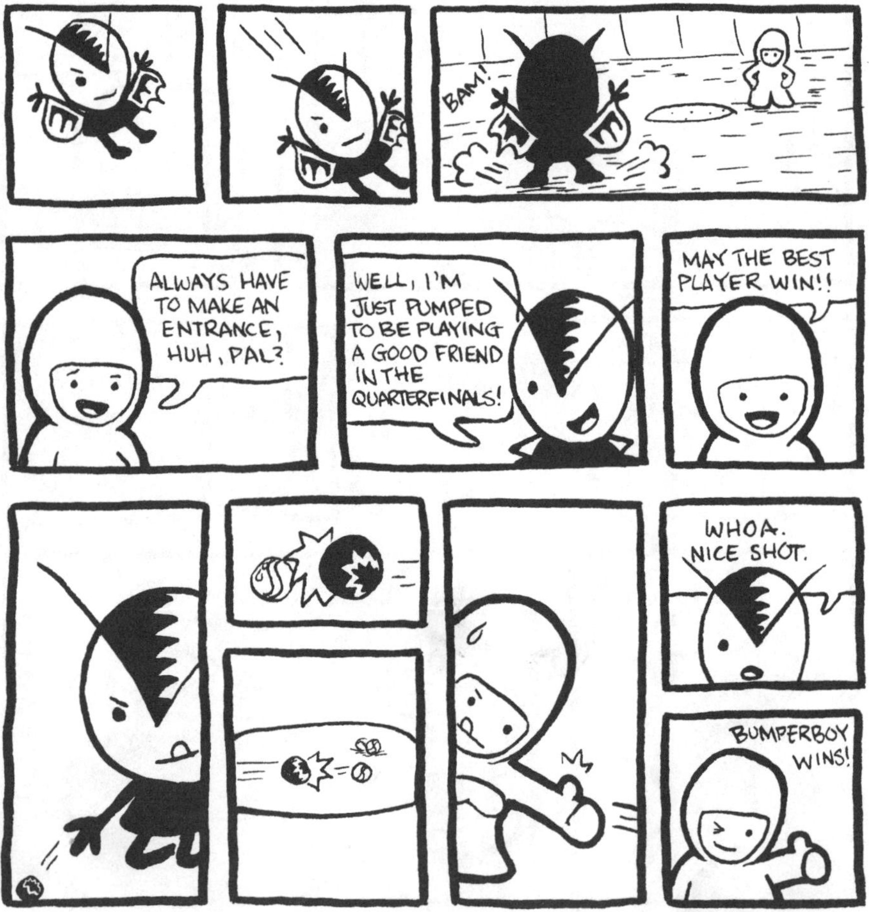
BAM!
ALWAYS HAVE TO MAKE AN ENTRANCE, HUH, PAL?
WELL, I'M JUST PUMPED TO BE PLAYING A GOOD FRIEND IN THE QUARTERFINALS!
MAY THE BEST PLAYER WIN!!
WHOA. NICE SHOT.
BUMPERBOY WINS!

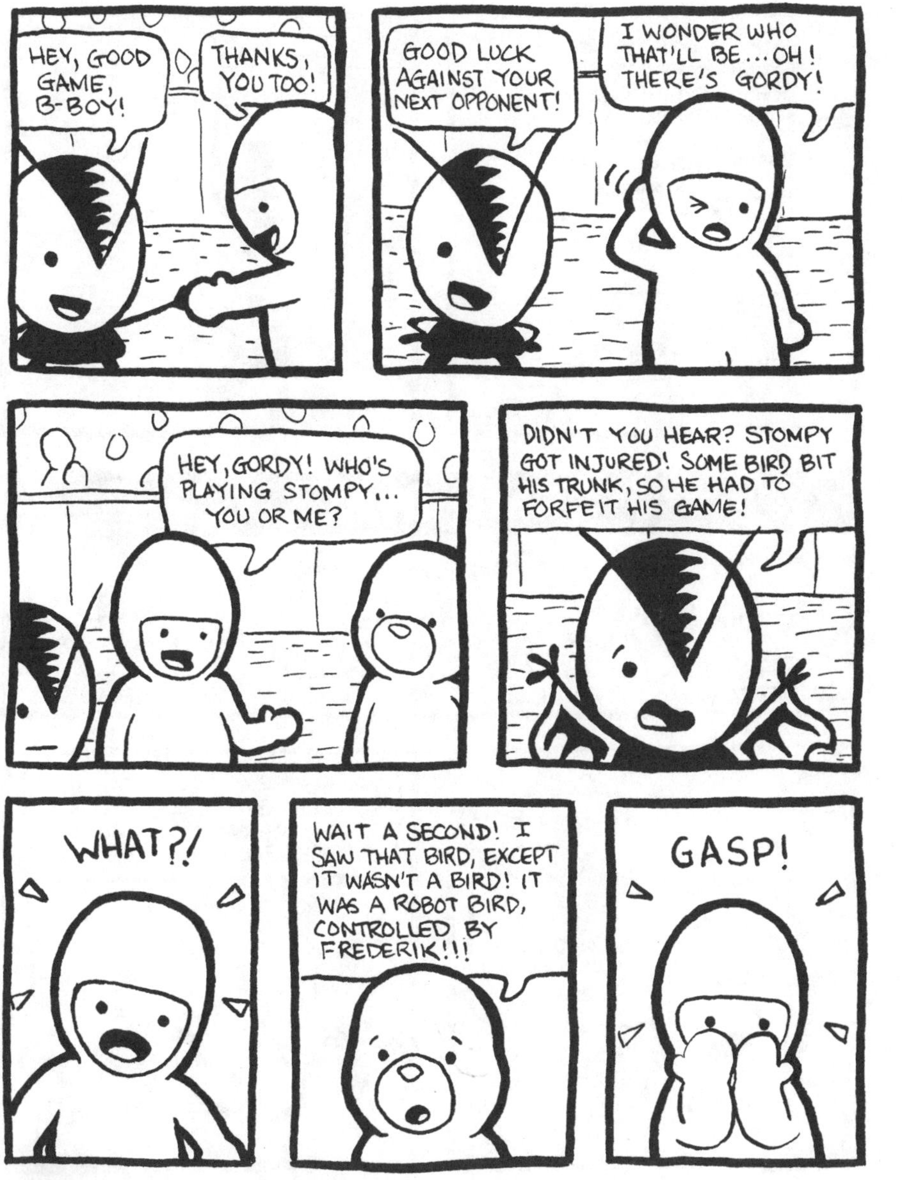
HEY, GOOD GAME, B-BOY!
THANKS, YOU TOO!
GOOD LUCK AGAINST YOUR NEXT OPPONENT!
I WONDER WHO THAT'LL BE... OH! THERE'S GORDY!
HEY, GORDY! WHO'S PLAYING STOMPY... YOU OR ME?
DIDN'T YOU HEAR? STOMPY GOT INJURED! SOME BIRD BIT HIS TRUNK, SO HE HAD TO FORFEIT HIS GAME!
WHAT?!
WAIT A SECOND! I SAW THAT BIRD, EXCEPT IT WASN'T A BIRD! IT WAS A ROBOT BIRD, CONTROLLED BY FREDERIK!!!
GASP!

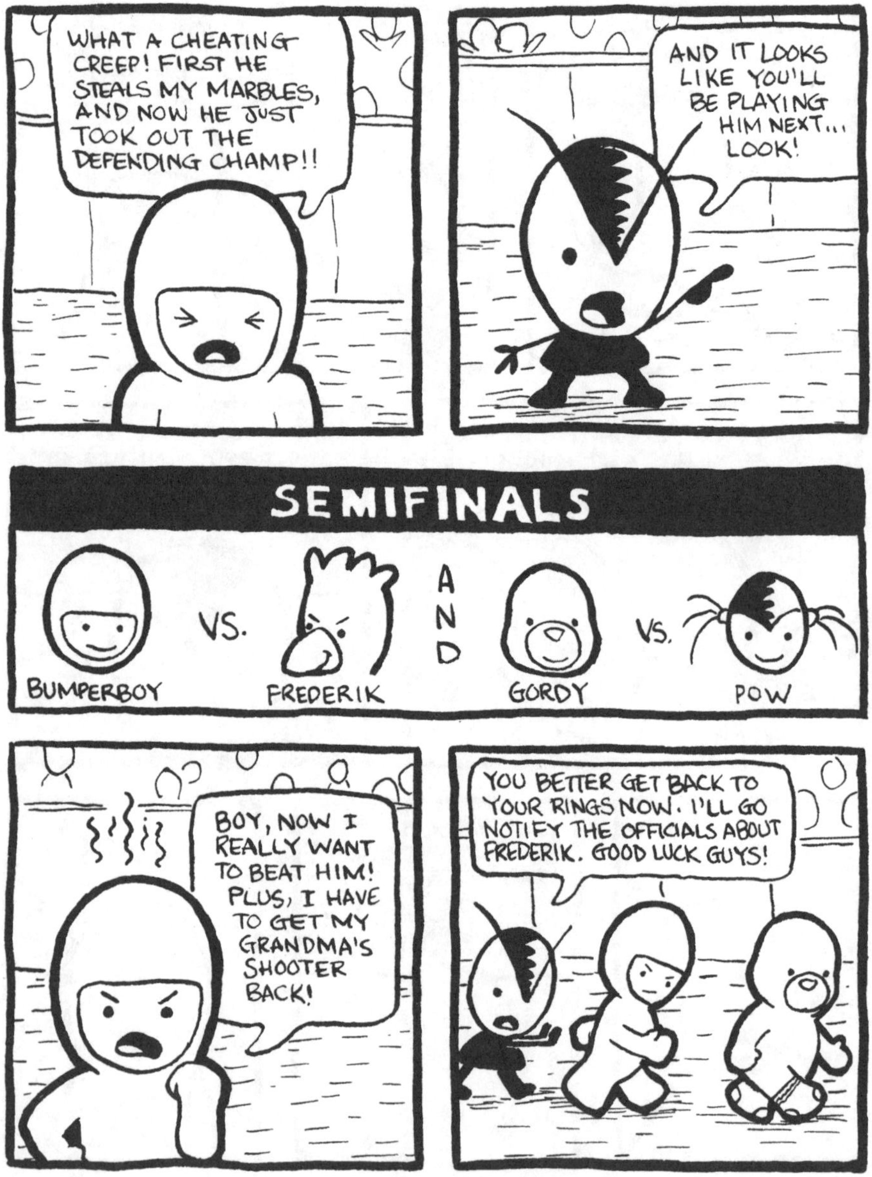
WHAT A CHEATING CREEP! FIRST HE STEALS MY MARBLES, AND NOW HE JUST TOOK OUT THE DEFENDING CHAMP!!
AND IT LOOKS LIKE YOU'LL BE PLAYING HIM NEXT... LOOK!
SEMIFINALS
BUMPERBOY
VS.
FREDERIK
AND
GORDY
VS.
POW
BOY, NOW I REALLY WANT TO BEAT HIM! PLUS, I HAVE TO GET MY GRANDMA'S SHOOTER BACK!
YOU BETTER GET BACK TO YOUR RINGS NOW. I'LL GO NOTIFY THE OFFICIALS ABOUT FREDERIK. GOOD LUCK GUYS!

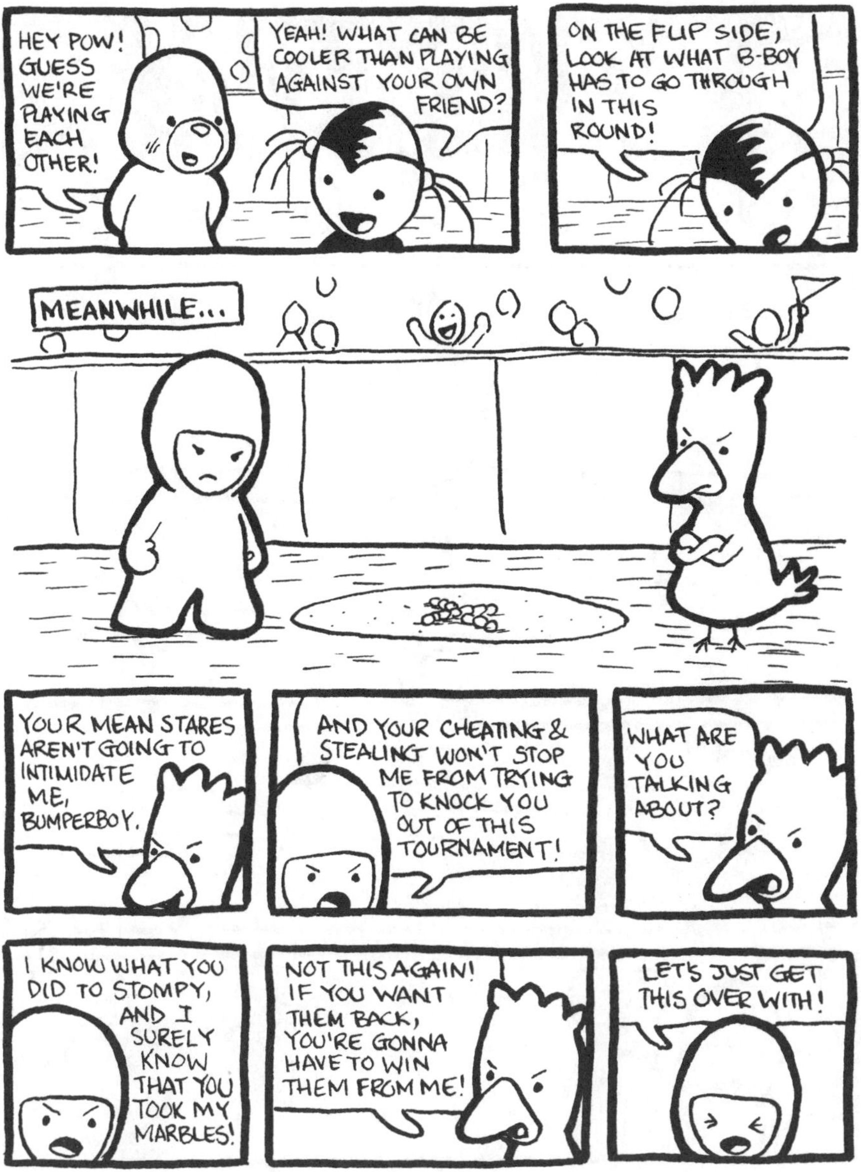
HEY POW! GUESS WE'RE PLAYING EACH OTHER!
YEAH! WHAT CAN BE COOLER THAN PLAYING AGAINST YOUR OWN FRIEND?
ON THE FLIP SIDE, LOOK AT WHAT B-BOY HAS TO GO THROUGH IN THIS ROUND!
MEANWHILE...
YOUR MEAN STARES AREN'T GOING TO INTIMIDATE ME, BUMPERBOY.
AND YOUR CHEATING & STEALING WON'T STOP ME FROM TRYING TO KNOCK YOU OUT OF THIS TOURNAMENT!
WHAT ARE YOU TALKING ABOUT?
I KNOW WHAT YOU DID TO STOMPY, AND I SURELY KNOW THAT YOU TOOK MY MARBLES!
NOT THIS AGAIN! IF YOU WANT THEM BACK, YOU'RE GONNA HAVE TO WIN THEM FROM ME!
LET'S JUST GET THIS OVER WITH!

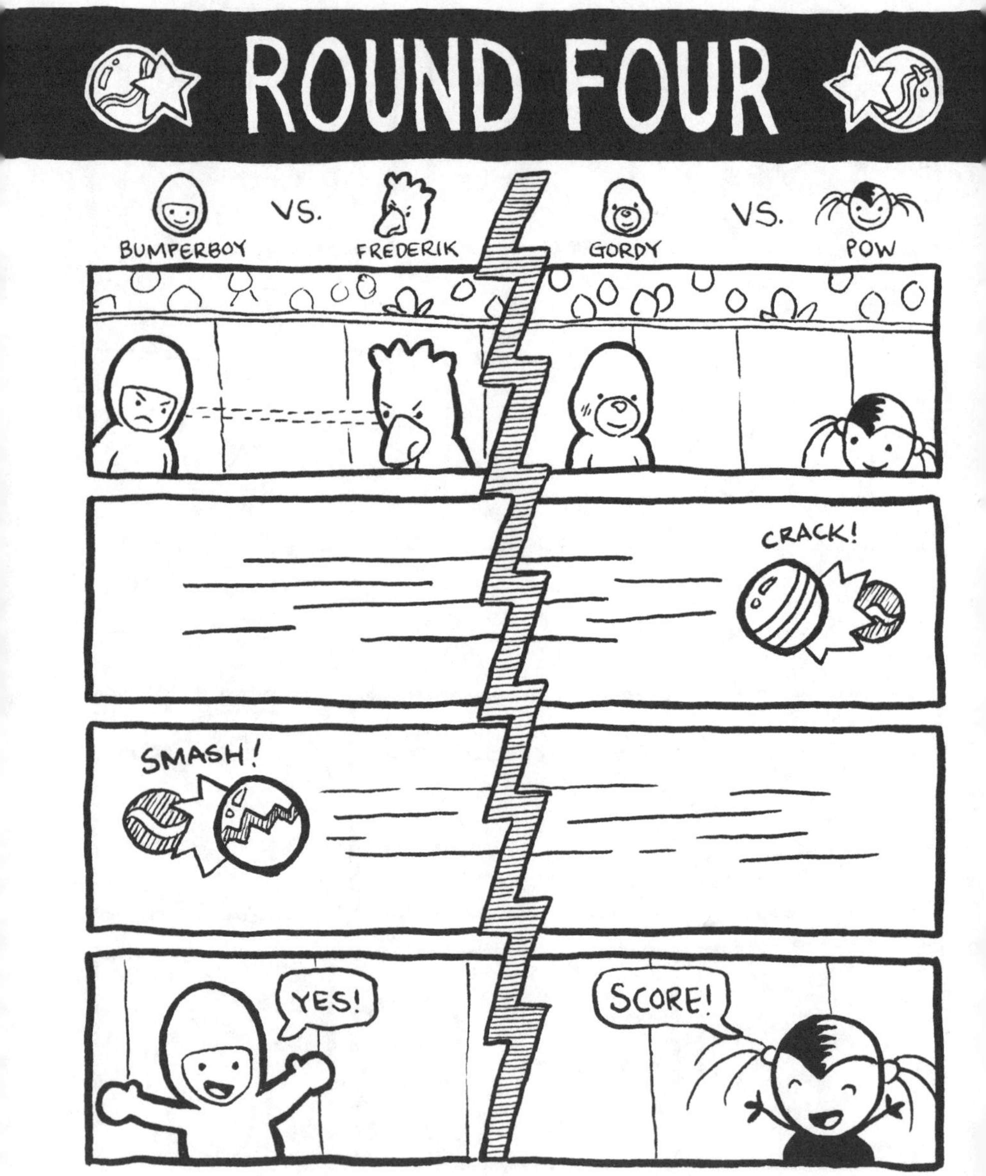
ROUND FOUR
BUMPERBOY
VS.
FREDERIK
GORDY
VS.
POW
CRACK!
SMASH!
YES!
SCORE!

ROUND FOUR

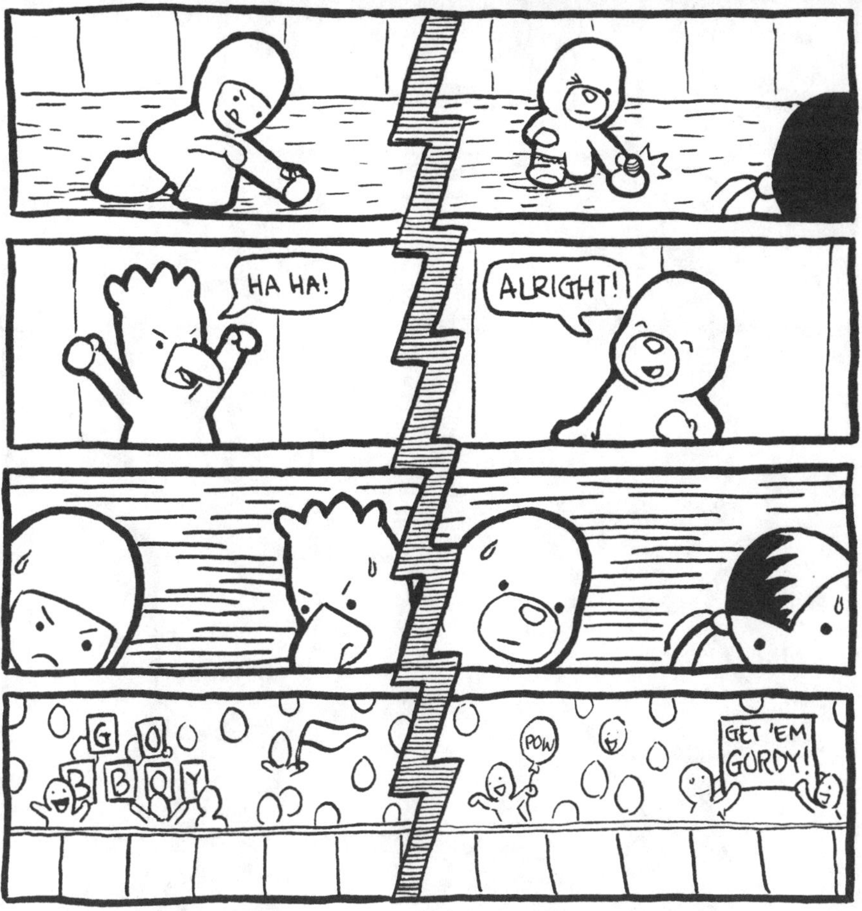
HA HA!
ALRIGHT!
GO
BBOY
POW
GET 'EM GURDY!

AND THE WINNERS ARE...

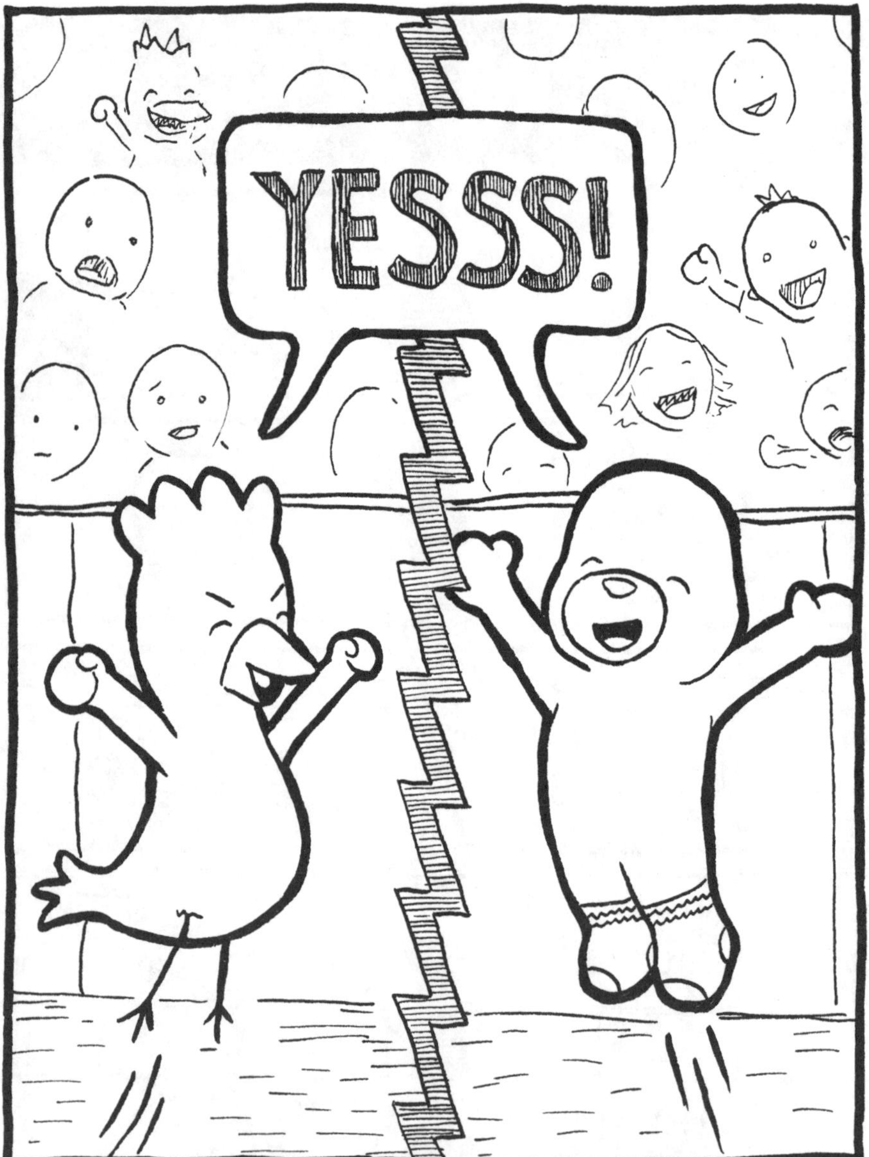
YESSS!

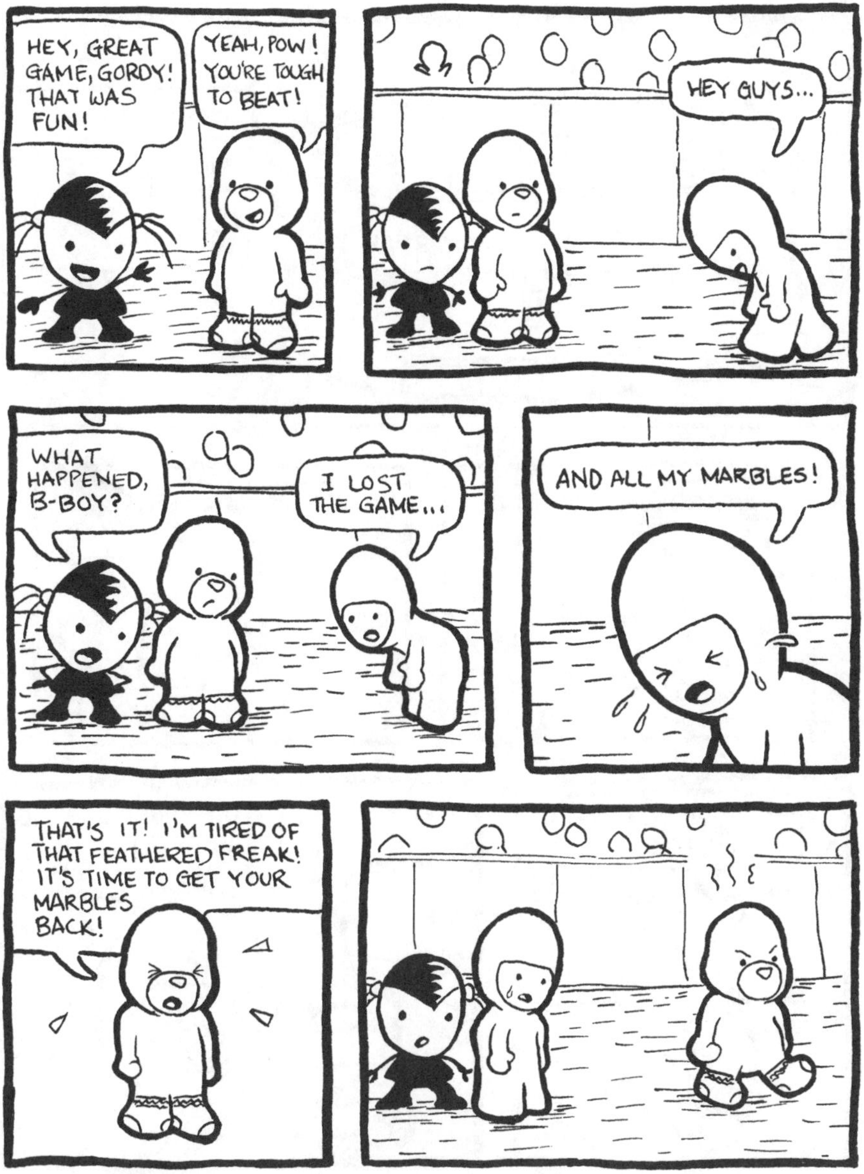
HEY, GREAT GAME, GORDY! THAT WAS FUN!
YEAH, POW! YOU'RE TOUGH TO BEAT!
HEY GUYS...
WHAT HAPPENED, B-BOY?
I LOST THE GAME...
AND ALL MY MARBLES!
THAT'S IT! I'M TIRED OF THAT FEATHERED FREAK! IT'S TIME TO GET YOUR MARBLES BACK!

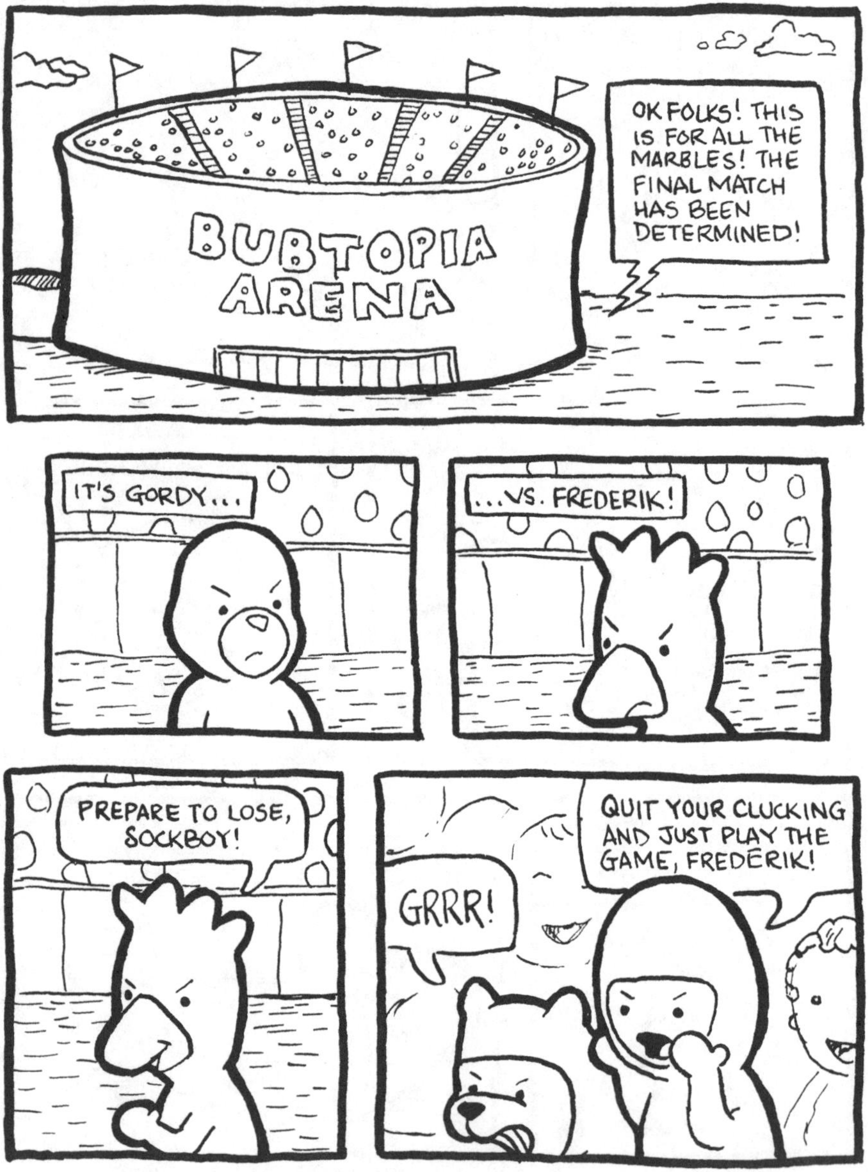
BUBTOPIA ARENA
OK FOLKS! THIS IS FOR ALL THE MARBLES! THE FINAL MATCH HAS BEEN DETERMINED!
IT'S GORDY...
...VS. FREDERIK!
PREPARE TO LOSE, SOCKBOY!
QUIT YOUR CLUCKING AND JUST PLAY THE GAME, FREDERIK!
GRRR!

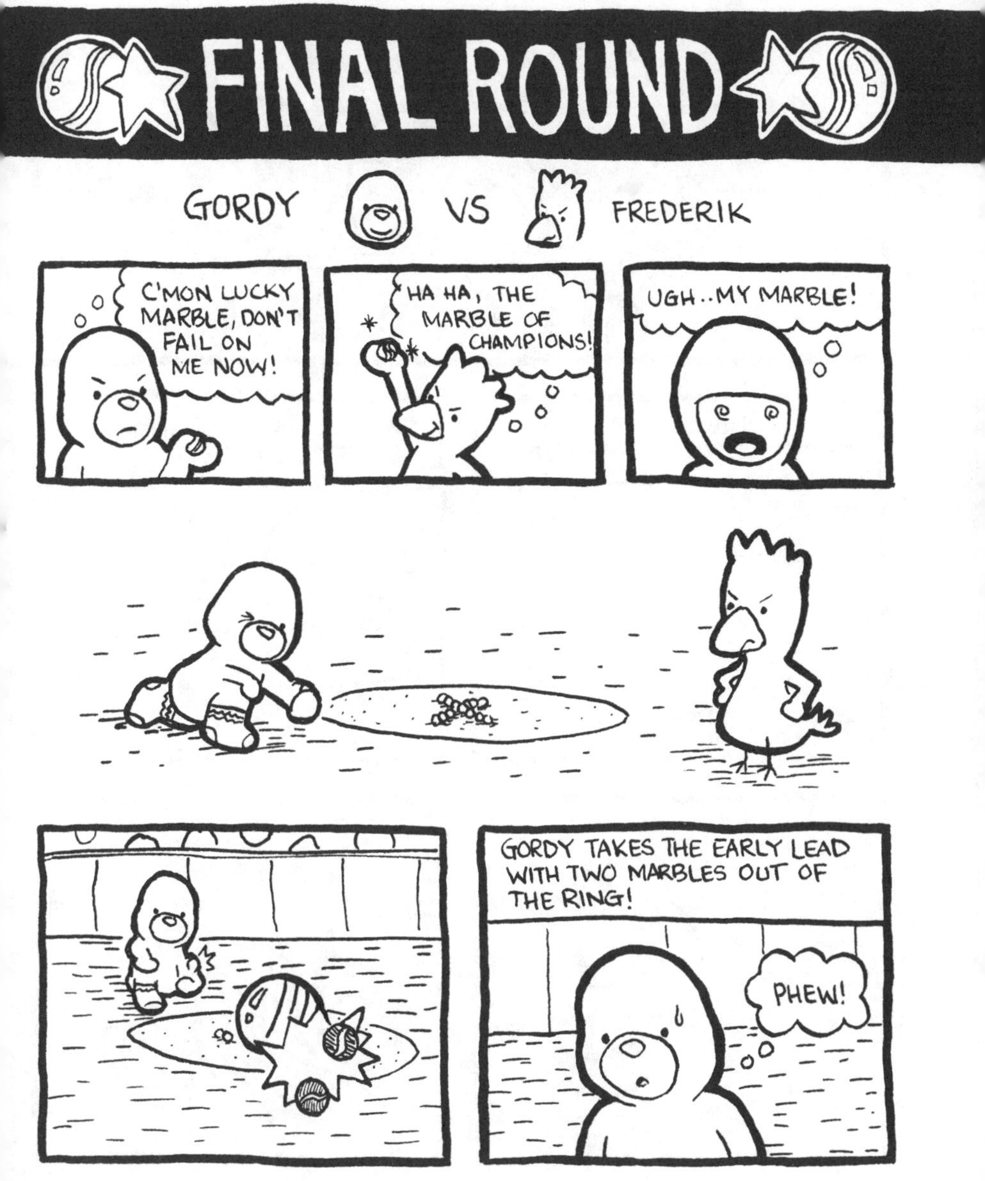
FINAL ROUND
GORDY VS FREDERIK
C'MON LUCKY MARBLE, DON'T FAIL ON ME NOW!
HA HA, THE MARBLE OF CHAMPIONS!
UGH..MY MARBLE!
GORDY TAKES THE EARLY LEAD WITH TWO MARBLES OUT OF THE RING!
PHEW!

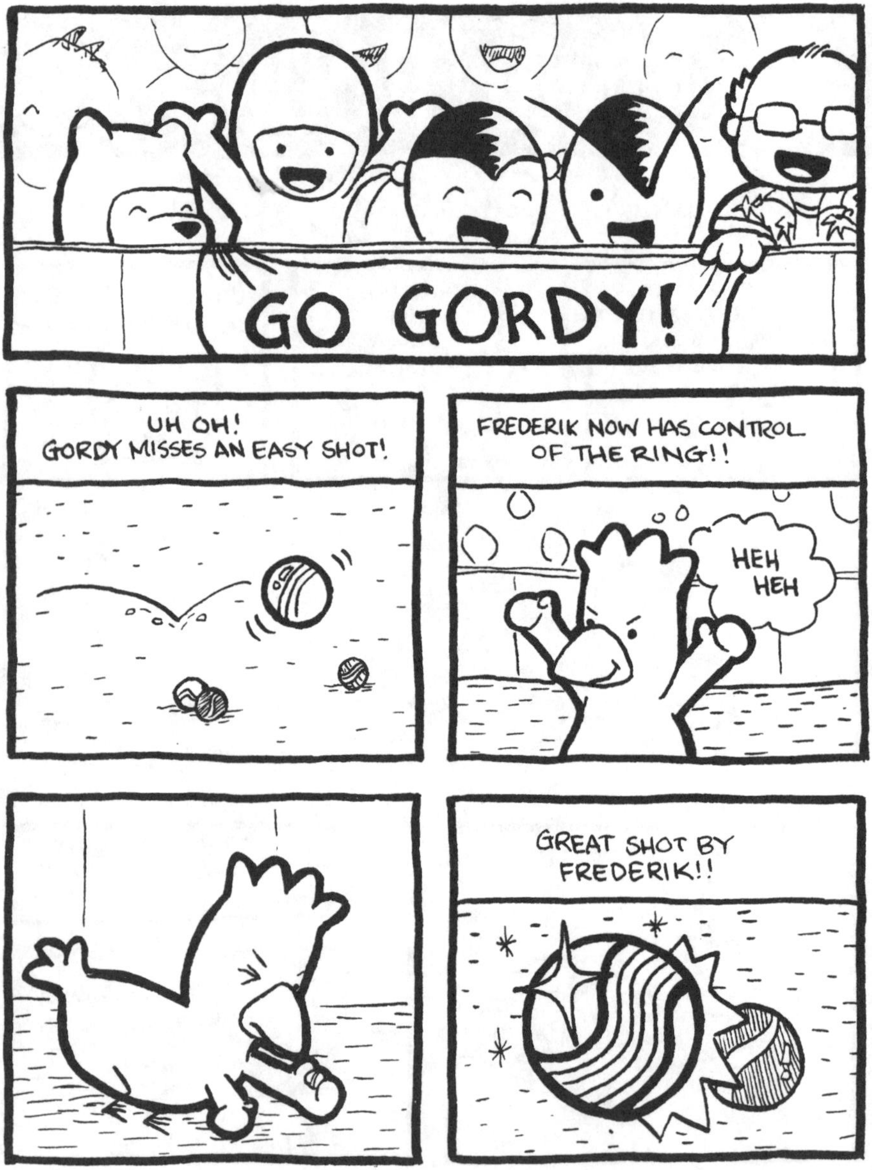
GO GORDY!
UH OH!
GORDY MISSES AN EASY SHOT!
FREDERIK NOW HAS CONTROL
OF THE RING!!
HEH
HEH
GREAT SHOT BY
FREDERIK!!

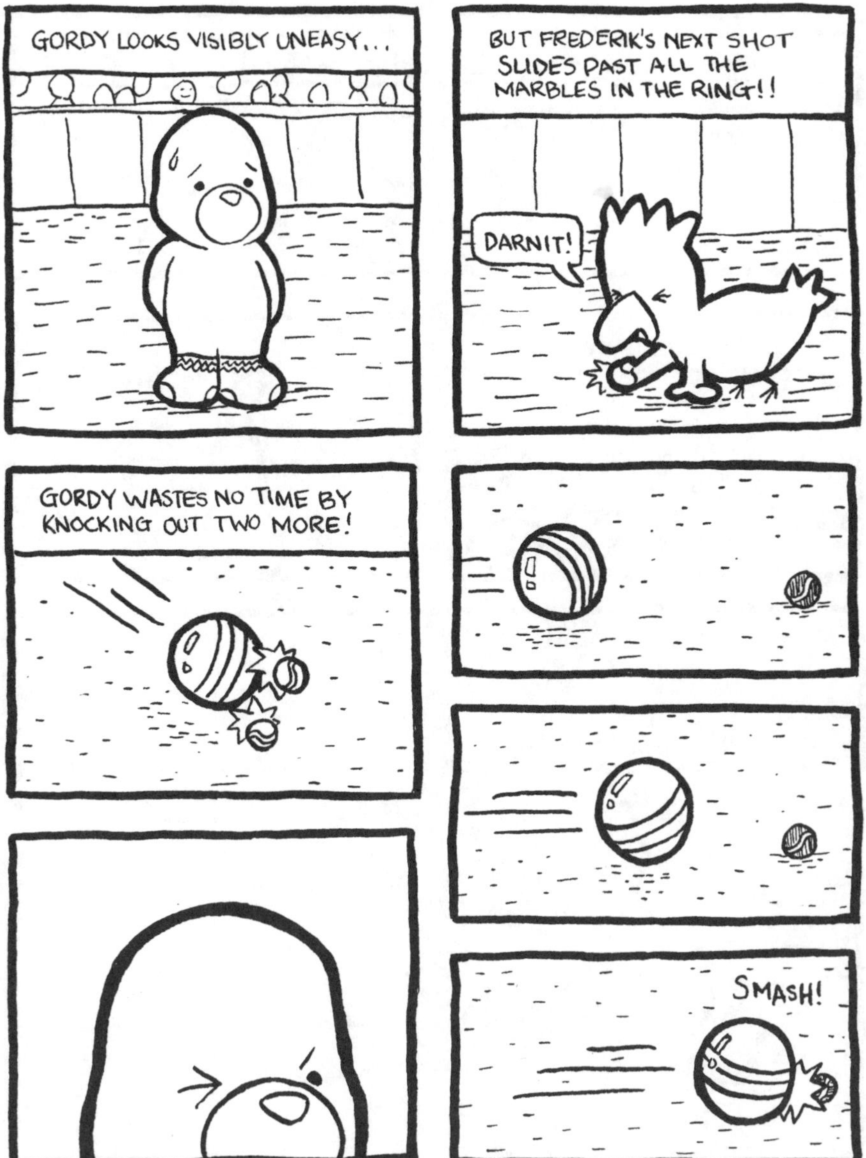
GORDY LOOKS VISIBLY UNEASY...
BUT FREDERIK'S NEXT SHOT SLIDES PAST ALL THE MARBLES IN THE RING!!
DARNIT!
GORDY WASTES NO TIME BY KNOCKING OUT TWO MORE!
SMASH!

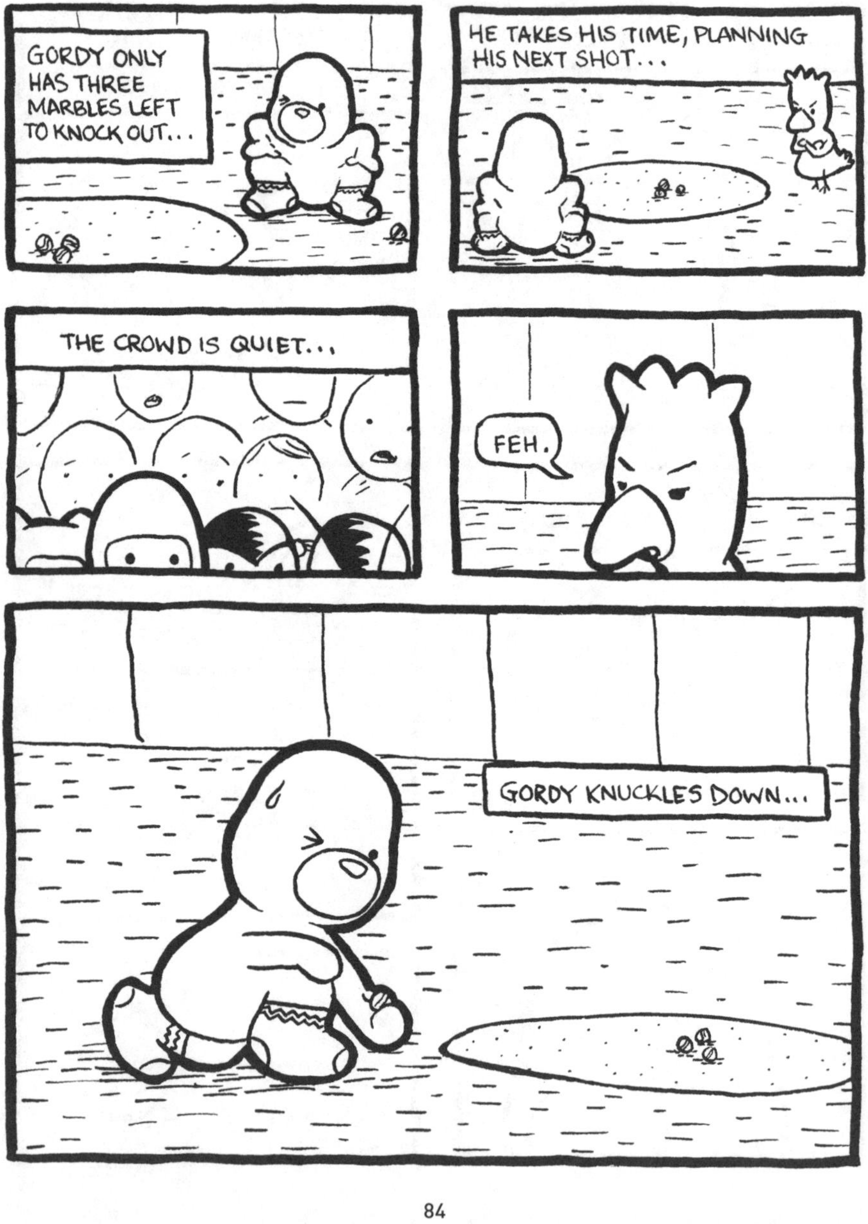
GORDY ONLY HAS THREE MARBLES LEFT TO KNOCK OUT...
HE TAKES HIS TIME, PLANNING HIS NEXT SHOT...
THE CROWD IS QUIET...
FEH.
GORDY KNUCKLES DOWN...

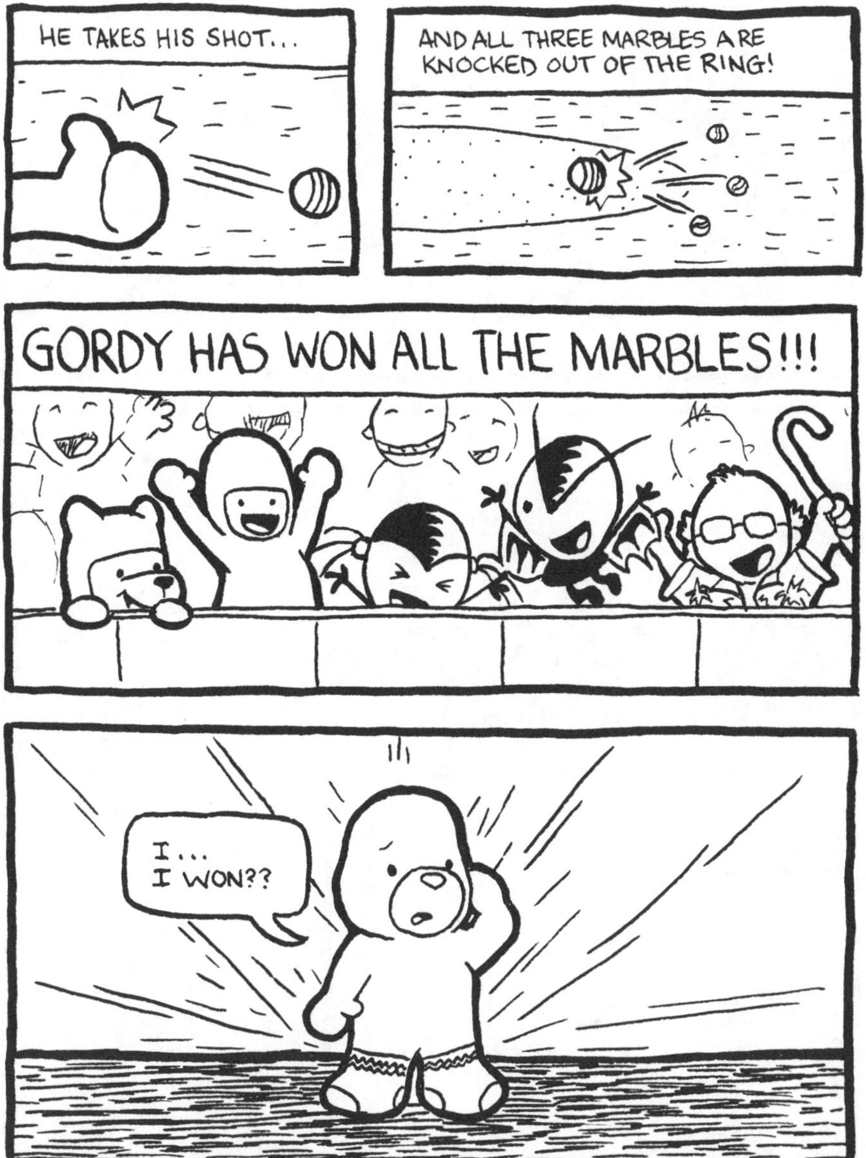
HE TAKES HIS SHOT...
AND ALL THREE MARBLES ARE KNOCKED OUT OF THE RING!
GORDY HAS WON ALL THE MARBLES!!!
I...
I WON??

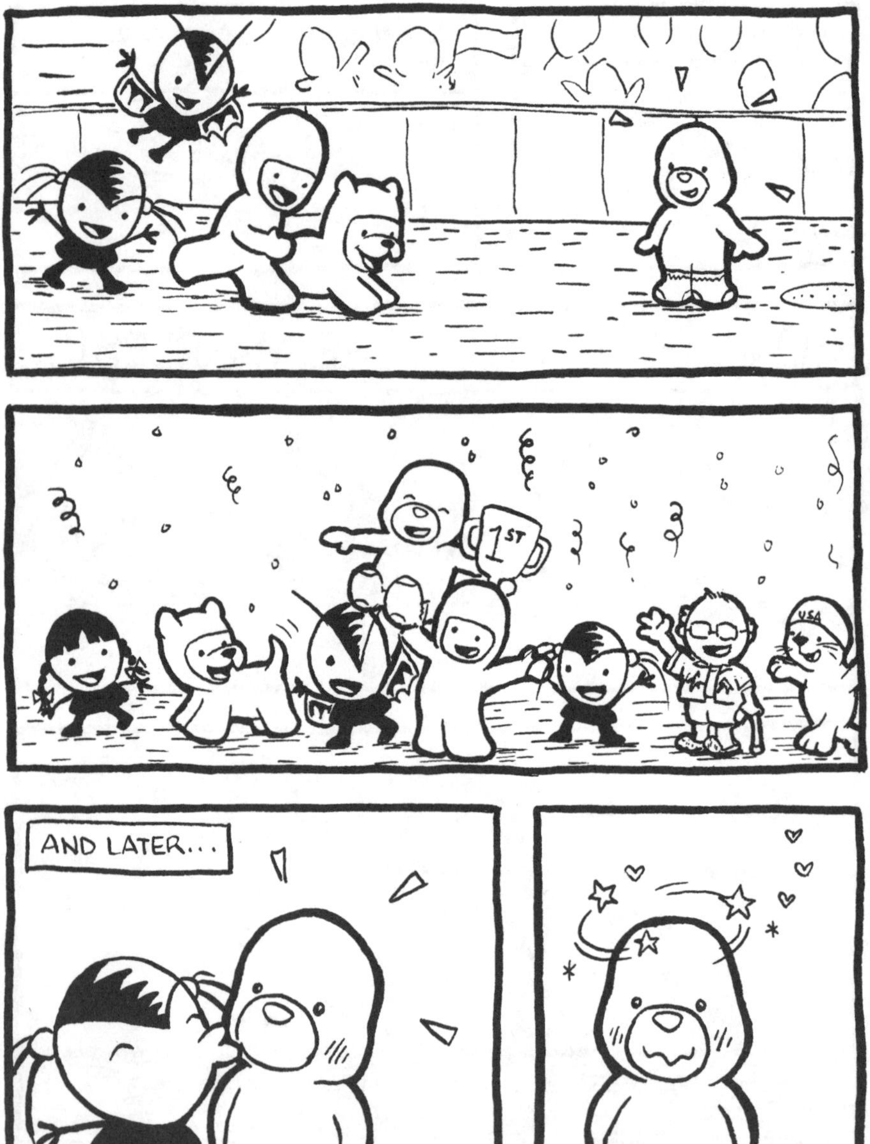
1ST
USA
AND LATER...

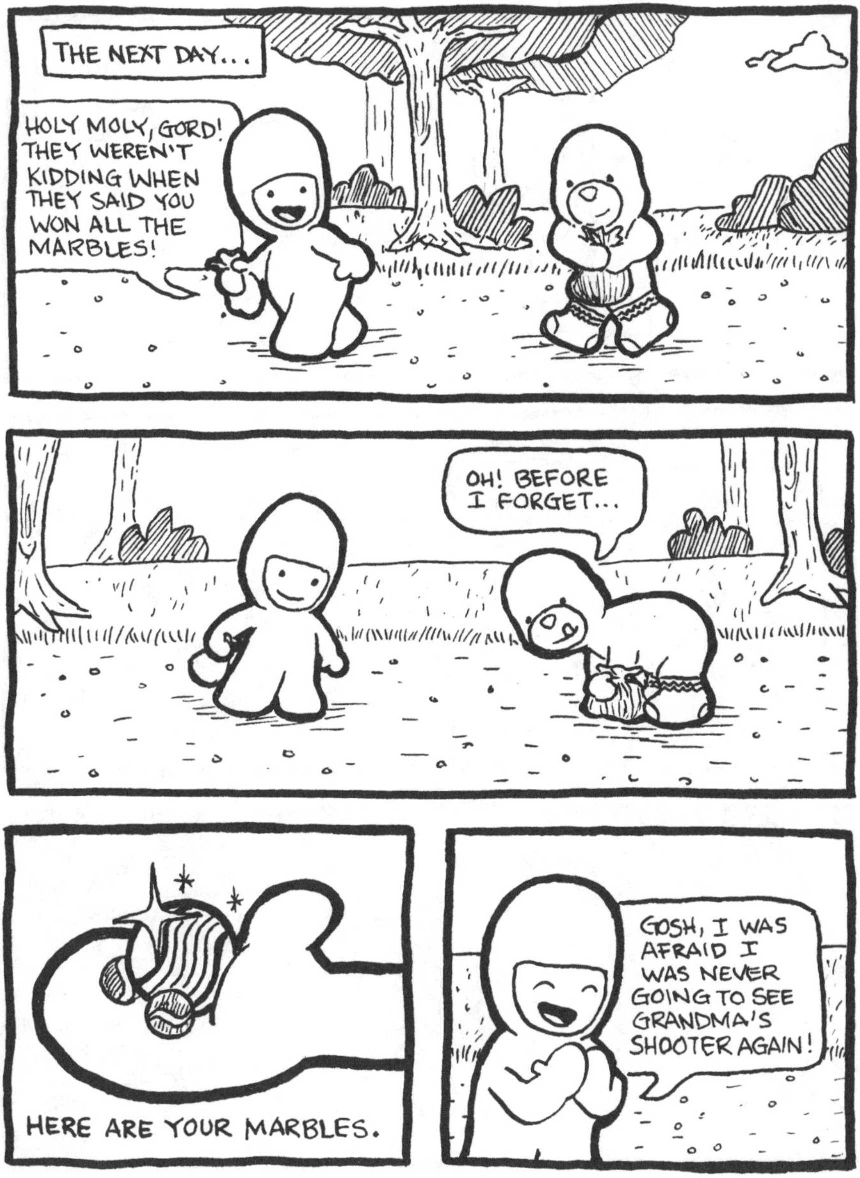
THE NEXT DAY...
HOLY MOLY, GORD! THEY WEREN'T KIDDING WHEN THEY SAID YOU WON ALL THE MARBLES!
OH! BEFORE I FORGET...
HERE ARE YOUR MARBLES.
GOSH, I WAS AFRAID I WAS NEVER GOING TO SEE GRANDMA'S SHOOTER AGAIN!

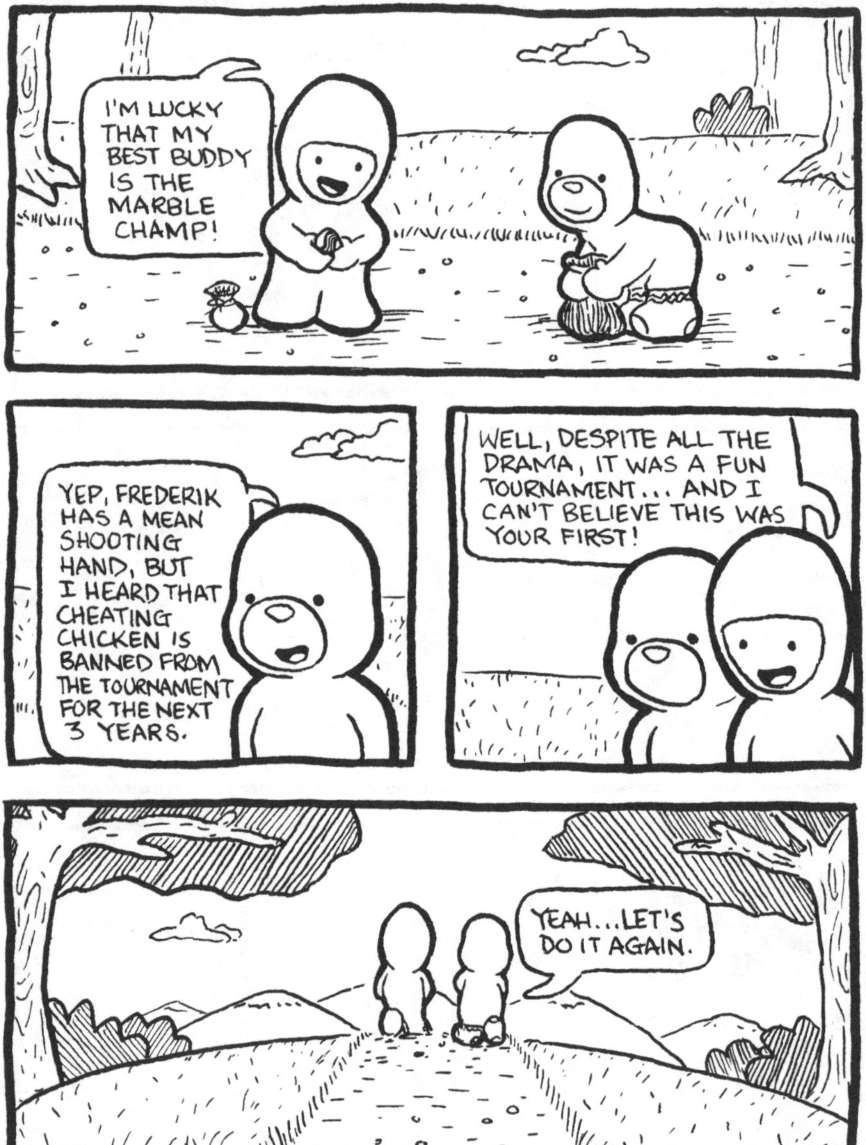
I'M LUCKY THAT MY BEST BUDDY IS THE MARBLE CHAMP!
YEP, FREDERIK HAS A MEAN SHOOTING HAND, BUT I HEARD THAT CHEATING CHICKEN IS BANNED FROM THE TOURNAMENT FOR THE NEXT 3 YEARS.
WELL, DESPITE ALL THE DRAMA, IT WAS A FUN TOURNAMENT... AND I CAN'T BELIEVE THIS WAS YOUR FIRST!
YEAH...LET'S DO IT AGAIN.

THE END

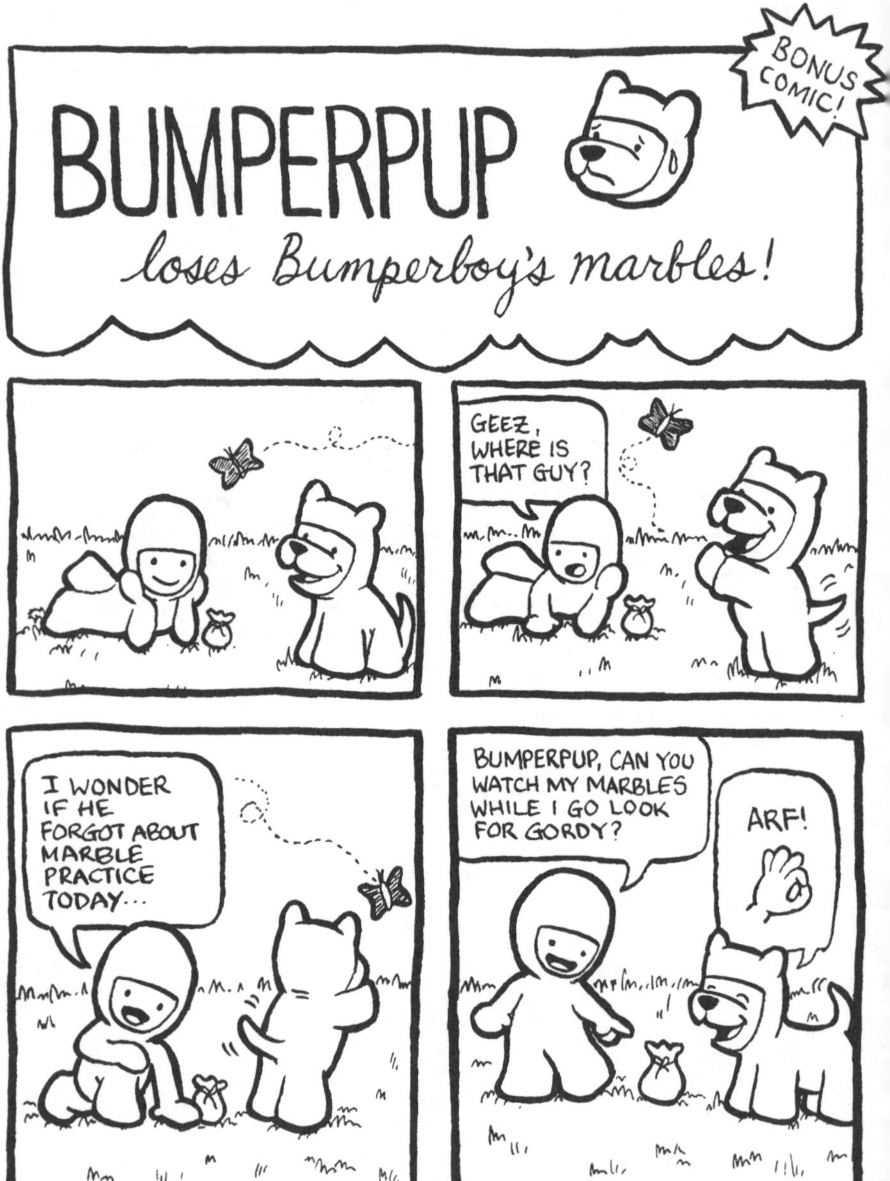
BONUS COMIC!
BUMPERPUP
loses Bumperboy's marbles!
GEEZ, WHERE IS THAT GUY?
I WONDER IF HE FORGOT ABOUT MARBLE PRACTICE TODAY...
BUMPERPUP, CAN YOU WATCH MY MARBLES WHILE I GO LOOK FOR GORDY?
ARF!

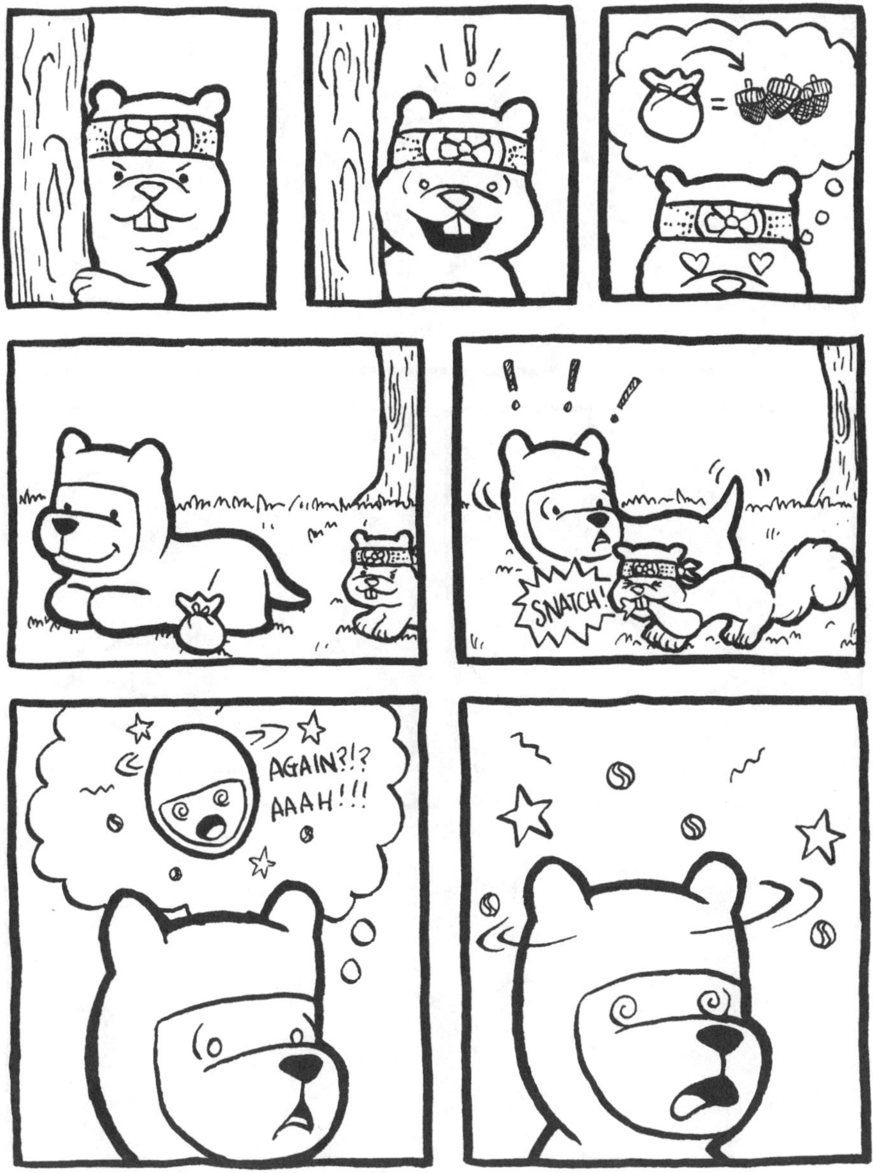

SNATCH!
AGAIN?!?
AAAH!!!

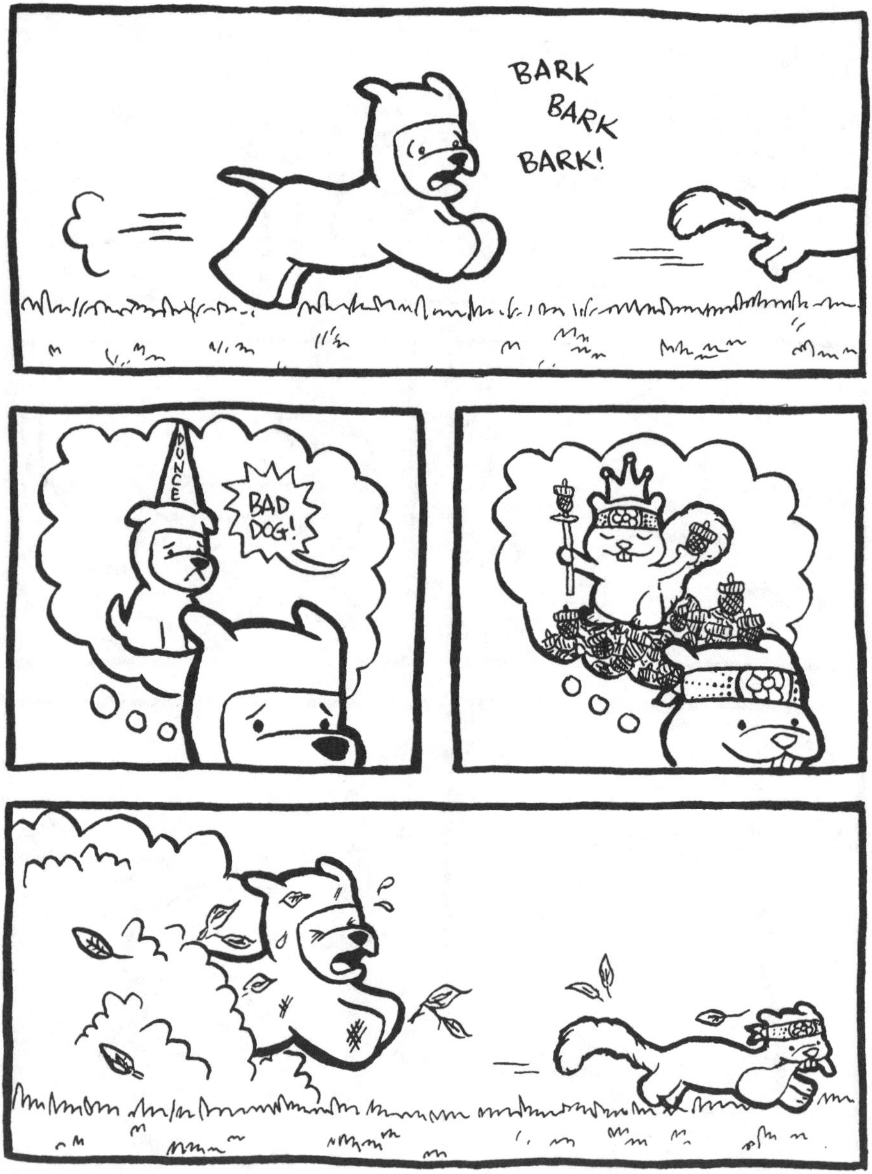
BARK
BARK
BARK!
DUNCE
BAD DOG!

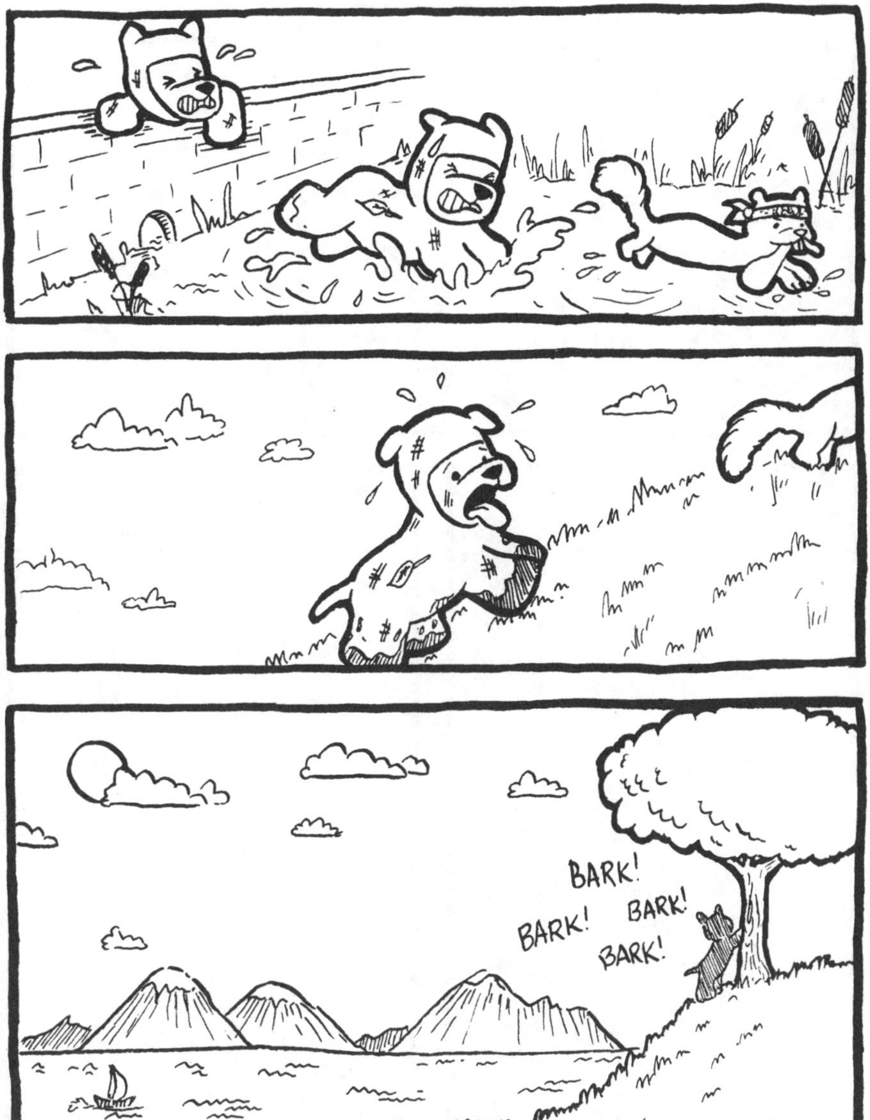
BARK!
BARK!
BARK!
BARK!

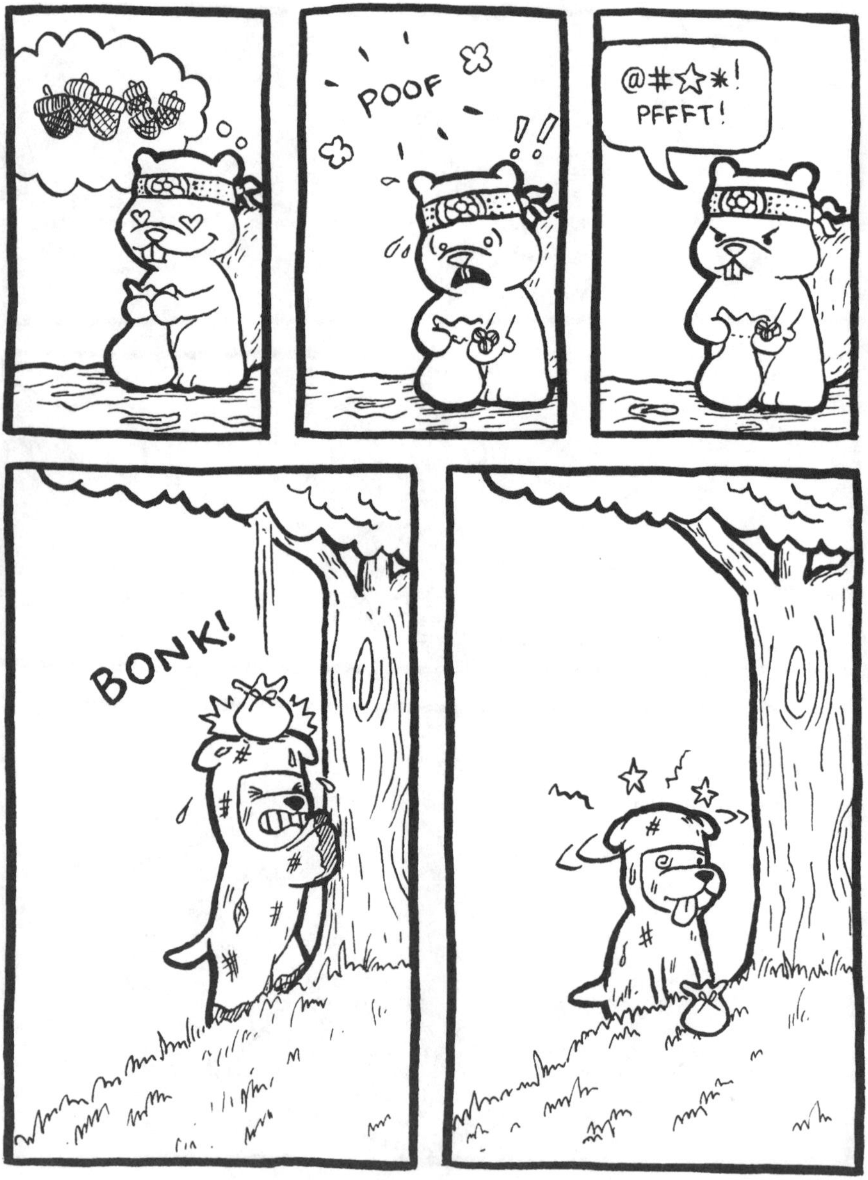
POOF
!!
@#☆*!
PFFFT!
BONK!

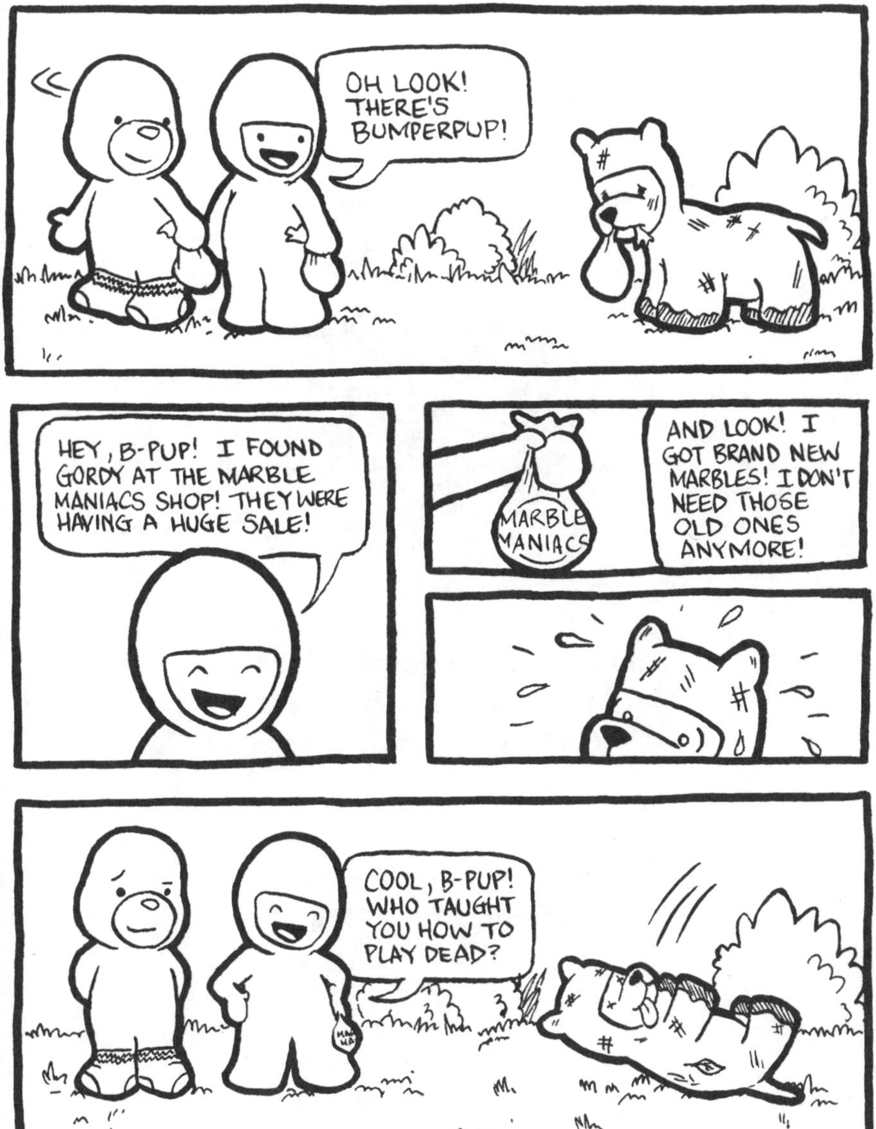
OH LOOK! THERE'S BUMPERPUP!
HEY, B-PUP! I FOUND GORDY AT THE MARBLE MANIACS SHOP! THEY WERE HAVING A HUGE SALE!
MARBLE MANIACS
AND LOOK! I GOT BRAND NEW MARBLES! I DON'T NEED THOSE OLD ONES ANYMORE!
COOL, B-PUP! WHO TAUGHT YOU HOW TO PLAY DEAD?
THE END

Westfield Memorial Library
Westfield, New Jersey

SEP 06

Be sure to visit **www.bumperboy.net**
for the latest news, Bumperboy
merchandise, Gordy's blog, and more!

www.bumperboy.net
debbie@bumperboy.net